OFF TRACK PLANET'S

SAN FRANCISCO

TRAVEL GUIDE

---------- *for the* ----------

YOUNG, SEXY,
= *and* = **BROKE**

BY THE EDITORS OF OTP

FREDDIE PIKOVSKY
ANNA STAROSTINETSKAYA

RUNNING PRESS
PHILADELPHIA · LONDON

© 2015 by Off Track Planet
Published by Running Press,
A Member of the Perseus Books Group

Books published by Running Press are available at special discounts for bulk
purchases in the United States by corporations, institutions, and other organizations.
For more information, please contact the Special Markets Department at the
Perseus Books Group, 2300 Chestnut Street, Suite 200, Philadelphia, PA 19103,
or call (800) 810-4145, ext. 5000, or e-mail special.markets@perseusbooks.com.

ISBN 978-0-7624-5711-3
Library of Congress Control Number: 2015934572

E-book ISBN 978-0-7624-5715-1

9 8 7 6 5 4 3 2 1
Digit on the right indicates the number of this printing

Cover design by Frances Soo Ping Chow
Interior design by Corinda Cook
Edited by Jordana Tusman
Typography: Archer, Bebas Neue, Mensch, Neutraface, Korolev

Running Press Book Publishers
2300 Chestnut Street
Philadelphia, PA 19103-4371

Visit us on the web!
www.runningpress.com

CONTENTS

INTRODUCTION

San Francisco is the golden nugget of California and has historically attracted creative, open-minded people who value lifestyle over status. It's small, but bursting with culture, nature, progressive politics, and quirk. From Japantown to the Irish populations of the Outerlands, the people of San Francisco are diverse and proud. The Mission is not just the birthplace of the super burrito, but a thriving Mexican community that's been around since before America's westward expansion. Chinatown isn't just a tourist attraction, but an enclave of Chinese descendants who staked their claim during the Gold Rush era. San Francisco's diverse residents have collectively pulled through disasters, pushed for progress in human rights, and continue to make strides in the fields of food, booze, and technology. Come here to ride cable cars down California Street, eat sourdough at Boudin, and ponder escape from Alcatraz, but once you've scratched the surface, we hope you leave with a little more substance under your nails.

This city has a lot to offer at every price point and is in constant flux: The rents are high; so many businesses share space in the form of pop-ups; there are food truck parks and one-night parties. While we sought out the best of the underground, know that many temporary businesses either fizzle out or establish brick-and-mortars. Our guide isn't traditional, because we're not in the business of spoon-feeding you information. The following section includes a few tips on how to get the most out of this book.

PREDEPARTURE

We created this section to give you the basics of what you'll need to know before you go. This includes general information about the weather, necessary paperwork like visas, available accommodations, transportation, and money-related issues. The biggest takeaway from this section is that transportation in San Francisco is going to be overwhelming at first, but you'll soon begin to see the web of wheels as a useful tool. Oh, and bring a sweater.

NEIGHBORHOODS

San Francisco is not only split into neighborhoods, but also microhoods, some with realtor-created names. It's possible for one city block to fall under several classifications and locals will argue with you until death about which neighborhood is which. For the purposes of this guide, we grouped some places together because they share similar vibes. For instance, downtown is broken up into the Tenderloin/Civic Center/Union Square and FiDi/Embarcadero chapters. On the other hand, we got as microscopic as was reasonable without driving you nuts, dedicating whole chapters to smaller neighborhoods like Bernal Heights and Hayes Valley. When in doubt about where something lies, look to hashtags for further classification of specific items, especially in the Richmond and Sunset chapters.

RECOMMENDATIONS

Every bar in San Francisco has excellent food and every café serves beer and wine. We explored San Francisco from all angles. Within each neighborhood, you'll find sections on cafés and bakeries, eateries, shopping options, things to see and do, and places to drink and party. The nonfunctional hashtags we threw in sum things up for those of you with little patience for full sentences; some are navigational cues and others are just plain silly. Keep in mind that prices for tickets, passes, festivals, and the like are subject to change as well, but are current as of the publication date of this guide.

HIPPIES

Northern California is known for its hippie population, and, sure, there are all kinds of hippies in San Francisco. Some of these hippies are filthy rich; others choose to live a simpler, dirtier life on the lawns of Golden Gate Park, on streets in the Haight, or across the bay in Berkeley. When you come here, don't be too quick to judge: You have the hippies to thank for being able to smoke weed freely on the street, talk about whatever the fuck crazy theories you want, and make out with the same sex without any sideways looks.

THINGS CHANGE

New businesses open and close in the same month. There are one-off parties, pop up bars and markets, and seasonal events. We did our best to cover what's current. If a listing in this guide no longer exists once you get there, don't fret; something will open down the street to fill the void.

Use this guide as a starting point to uncover the hidden treasures of this beautiful city. We encourage you to try every burrito in the Mission and every cocktail in SOMA. Talk to the hippies in the Haight, and pop a few historic mochi in Japantown. Hike up every hill to give yourself a new perspective on the city and let it make you fall in love with life.

A BRIEF HISTORY

San Franciscans, as mellow and earth-loving as they seem, don't take any shit; not from the government, not in the face of human inequality, not even from natural disasters. As a culturally and monetarily rich city, San Francisco's story revolves around innovation and the criminals, hippies, and tech nerds who made it all happen.

San Francisco did not begin with the Gold Rush. Native Americans occupied the Bay Area until conquistadors "discovered" the land. In 1769, Gaspar de Portola established the Presidio and announced that there was whaling and seafood wrangling to be done. The native Ohlone tribe was used to build structures for the Spanish, including the Misíon de San Francisco de Asís, until they died out from disease brought over by Spain and were subsequently buried under that mission (now called Mission Dolores, aka "Mission of Pain"). With the natives dead, the Spanish struggled to develop this new-found land, were grossed out by the rats and fleas, and left it in Mexico's care when the country gained its independence from Spain in 1821. Mexico made the best of the land and it flourished.

Around 1826, Jedediah Smith and company started poking around over the Sierra Nevadas, illegally entering California to look for beaver. Claiming it was their "manifest destiny," Americans planned for westward expansion, forcing Mexico to sell the land after the Mexican-American War.

Newly renamed, San Francisco had potential, but James Marshall's discovery of gold in 1848 at Sutter's Mill in Coloma started a mad rush for money. The influx of greedy gold diggers in 1849 (the '49ers) ballooned the city's population from 800 to 25,000 within

1776
Misíon San Francisco de Asís (aka Mission Dolores) is founded

one year. But the city itself (a few miles up from Sutter's Mill) was a ghost town when the mines were hot. Once personal fortunes were made, miners went back to the city to wait for their ships at the ports. What happens when a bunch of young, money-hungry, horny dudes overrun a place?

The Barbary Coast (present-day Fisherman's Wharf and North Beach) was an area full of miners, hookers, drunks, gamblers, and criminals, who made their living gold digging (and later stealing). The area became an intoxicated playground with a formidable red-light district. Boatloads of international opportunists came from Ireland, Australia, Japan, and China. Once the gold was sucked dry, those with nuggets became targets. The (pretty racist) term *shanghaied* came from this era where "crimpers" would slip a little poison into drinks at saloons, load people on ships, and rob them blind before tossing them into the bay.

While some took to the mines, others (like the Chinese) accepted low-wage jobs to serve the booming population. When the

Trailblazer Jedediah Smith plans for westward expansion, forcing Mexicans to sell their land
1826

A massive 8.0 earthquake wipes out most of the city's structures
1906

1848
James Marshall's discovery of gold starts a mad rush for money

gold was gone and the Chinese were left standing, profiting quietly on the sidelines of the Gold Rush, resentment from those who busted quickly grew.

Then Henry Comstock discovered silver ore in 1859 and a new rush was ignited. The now-hated Chinese were hired to build the Transcontinental Railroad, completed in 1869, to facilitate faster greedy travel. The Chinese Exclusion Acts were put into effect to deny further Chinese immigration, exclude Chinese residents from jobs, and bar them from housing.

The influx of new money turned into a land grab. Residential mansions, historic buildings, fancy restaurants, and bars were built to serve the pompous new community, and cable cars were set up in 1873 to cart them around the hills. Activists strived to preserve the natural beauty of the area and public projects were built, notably Buena Vista Park in 1894 and the failed Sutro Baths. But

Mother Nature had different plans for the city's restructuring.

Disaster struck in 1906 when a massive 8.0 earthquake wiped out most of the city's structures, caused widespread fires for three days, and left a third of San Francisco's population homeless, and countless dead. All the riches burned and the city crumbled.

But it made a quick comeback and people began to rebuild and restore. New structures included the Great American Music Hall (1907), Coit Tower (1933), and the Golden Gate Bridge (1937). The Barbary Coast was burned down and a new tourist-attracting port, called Fisherman's Wharf, was built in its place. Alcatraz Island floated in the distance, housing Al Capone from 1934 until 1938.

San Francisco began gaining popularity as the major port of the West, and then came the 1941 Japanese attack on Pearl Harbor in Hawaii. While many Japanese citizens were ordered to internment camps elsewhere in

Golden Gate
Bridge opens
1937

1934
Alcatraz houses
Al Capone from
1934-1938

1957
Jack Kerouac's Beat
movement grows,
with writers and poets
settling in North Beach

the country, in San Francisco the JACL (Japanese American Citizens League) was formed in resistance and successfully retained for Japanese Americans in SF their rights to live freely.

San Francisco was quickly turning into a place of respite for those who thought differently, had antiauthoritarian values, and felt free to explore their sexuality. Jack Kerouac's *On the Road* (1957) described the westward journey of freethinkers, and the Beat movement grew, settling in North Beach, where they sipped coffee at Trieste, wrote poetry, wore black, and rhythmically snapped their fingers.

FUN FACT

Alcatraz appears on every list of the most haunted places on Earth. Whenever people go looking for ghosts on the desolate island, they tend to find them.

All this weirdness drove the government's search for communists to the Bay Area in the late '50s. But San Franciscans weren't having it. UC Berkeley students organized a famous protest against blacklisting and the police turned hoses on them; this ignited a fire within the souls of peace-seeking residents. When the '60s hit, hippies arose from the watery streets.

How did beatniks turn into hippies? It was called the acid test. The author of *One Flew Over the Cuckoo's Nest*, Ken Kesey, threw LSD parties, soundtracked by the Grateful Dead, that expanded the up-for-anything minds of the Beat population to create swirly, colorful hippies. The Vietnam War was on the horizon and the laid-back hippies of SF were going to fight it with love (and a bunch of drugs). In 1967, the Summer of Love, with its slogan "Make love, not war," turned into a citywide peaceful protest of free music, food, and humping concentrated in the Haight. All was groovy until people's free love turned into widespread disease, the Hell's Angels broke loose, and demented killers, like Charles Manson, broke up the party.

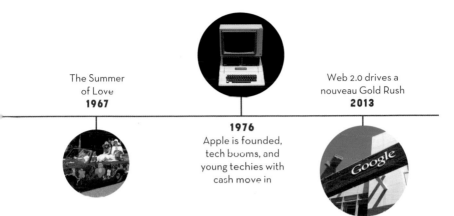

The Summer
of Love
1967

1976
Apple is founded,
tech booms, and
young techies with
cash move in

Web 2.0 drives a
nouveau Gold Rush
2013

The Haight went to shit during the '70s, and while some old hippies stayed, many dispersed to other parts of the city. The gays moved over to the Castro, with proud rainbow flags and wild disco parties that attracted others who wanted to be "out and proud." The Castro was a haven for those normally persecuted elsewhere. Gay government officials were elected, most notably Harvey Milk, whose assassination bound the neighborhood together in both mourning and a united push toward progress. While the AIDS epidemic hit the Castro hard, united residents quickly rallied for better health care and the development of vaccinations.

Business-minded hippies moved to Silicon Valley when the Haight fell apart. By the '80s, those with cash started thinking about ways to reinvigorate industry, and clunky, expensive computers were born to serve businesses. Others, like Steve Jobs, started tinkering with mind-bending projects in their garages, with the goal of bringing free information to the masses. Investors eventually caught on and tech boomed. Young developers suddenly had cash and moved into places like SOMA and the Mission, and real estate developers followed. Eventually, the price of information created a conflict between investors and tech developers and the bubble burst in 2000, leaving young tech junkies jobless. The population of San Francisco dropped drastically.

The development of Web 2.0 created new tech opportunities and reinvigorated Silicon Valley, drawing new entrepreneurs from all over the world, looking to strike it rich. But this nouveau Gold Rush did not come without consequences.

As evidenced by the 2013 Google Bus riots, residents (especially in the Mission) are currently worried that they will be displaced, and SF's distinct cultural pockets will be wiped out if real estate developers continue to serve the whims of new money.

History seems to repeat itself in San Francisco, and there is nothing more dangerous than a twenty-two-year-old with a million dollars in his pocket. But given the city's hard-fighting history, San Franciscans will be sure to pull through victorious, adding a new layer to their kaleidoscope of culture.

PREDEPARTURE

It may be small, but San Francisco can be overwhelming at first with its BART, rails, buses, streetcars, and cable cars. We're here to give you some pointers on transportation, general health and safety, and accommodations, and a little insight into SF's liberal—but loud—culture and politics so you can navigate these hills with ease.

VISAS AND DOCS

VISAS

For short visits (ninety days or less), the residents of thirty-seven countries fall under the "visa waiver program" and do not need to obtain a visa to enter the United States. Beginning in 2006, the passports from these countries came with an integrated chip that permits entrance without the need for additional documentation. Check the U.S. Department of State's website to see if your country is on the list.

If you happen to be from, say, Mexico, consider yourself fucked. To get into the United States for any period of time, you'll need to apply for a visa. You first have to fill out Form DS-160, upload a photo, and arrange an interview with your local U.S. embassy (to which you'll need to bring the confirmation page of Form DS-160, a $160 application fee, and an additional issuance fee, if applicable).

Longer visits require travelers to apply for certain visas based on their intended purpose in the United States. For all work visas with a known departure time, your prospective employer must submit a petition for your work visa and go through the process with you.

To study in the States, you must obtain an F-1 or M-1 visa prior to your arrival. Generally, once you are accepted into a U.S. school, you will be entered into SEVIS (Student and Exchange Visitor Information System) and will need to fill out several forms and pay the I-901 SEVIS fee of $200 (which you can pay online). To obtain your student visa, you have to fill out all applicable forms, pay fees, and go through an interview. All student visa information can be found on the U.S. Department of State's website.

DOCUMENTS

Regardless of your destination, always travel with copies of your passport, prescriptions, and birth certificate. Emailing these to yourself is also a good safety precaution.

TRANSPORTATION

FROM THE AIRPORT

The two major airports that service the East Bay are San Francisco International (SFO) and Oakland International (OAK). At SFO, hopping on the terminal stop of the BART will get you to any part of the city in thirty to forty minutes and the cost of the ticket is calculated based on distance ($8–$10 to get downtown). From OAK, you'll need to board the BART to OAK shuttle ($6) and ride it out to the Coliseum BART station and then proceed to San Francisco BART stations. A cab ride will cost you about $60 from SFO to downtown SF and there's always Uber and Lyft if you're lazy.

San Jose Mineta International (SJC) sits at the bottom of the peninsula. If you fly into this airport, the VTA Airport Flyer (a free shuttle) takes you to the CalTrain station. From there, you can ride the train into the city.

CALTRAIN

The Caltrain station is at Fourth and King Streets, near AT&T Park, and the route is divided into six zones, connecting the small counties of the Bay Area. Tickets must be purchased at the station prior to boarding, and fares are calculated based on distance.

BART

BART is a funny little train and "Take BART . . . and you're there" is its funny little slogan. BART (Bay Area Rapid Transit) is SF's version of a subway and feels like the airtrain at Disneyland. It's clunky and confusing at first, but it will get you around the major parts of the city (and the East Bay) relatively fast. There are five rainbow-colored lines, each with only a handful of stops. Each line is named after its terminal station (which will appear on the arrival screens when the train is pulling in).

The kiosks (which will accept cash or credit) at BART stations have the following options: You can either buy a $20 card or add (or subtract) $1 or $0.05 in value until you reach the amount you'd like to load on your card. You swipe your new card in and fares are calculated based on the distance once you swipe out at your destination. It's cumbersome, but it'll work out after a few tries. But what if you swipe in and don't have

enough to get out? To avoid the mass panic of people being stuck in the station, there are add fare machines (that often only take small denominations of cash) to help you get out of the red. Also, attendants are usually on duty on one side of the station.

OTP Tip: BART shuts down at midnight, so if you're partying far from home, prepare to pay for an expensive cab ride to your bed or spend an awkward night in someone else's. There is an all-night OWL bus, but it's more of a homeless cruise than anything else.

MUNI

The MUNI system consists of buses, Metro light rail, streetcars, and cable cars. This system crisscrosses all of San Francisco, obviating the need to use your feet.

BUSES

Almost every intersection in SF has at least one bus stop. Some are fancy, with digital displays indicating the arrival time of the next bus (tip: They're not always right), while others are just yellow strips with numbers written on telephone poles. Fare is $2.25 and you must have exact change. You'll be handed a transfer that's good for ninety minutes, which means you can take another bus (or five) for the next hour and a half.

METRO LIGHT RAIL

This part of the system consists of six rail lines. They are: J (Church), KT (Ingleside), L (Taraval), M (Ocean), N (Judah), and S (Castro Shuttle). Fares and transfers work the same way as buses. Metro stations are underground along Market Street but then pop outside for the remainder of their routes. You can check arrival times on the SFMTA site.

OTP Tip: Many bus, rail, and cable car stops are positioned right in the middle of the street. Don't be afraid to stand in traffic.

STREETCARS

MUNI puts different vintage streetcars on one route (the F line that runs from Fisherman's Wharf to Embarcadero, down Market, and up to the Castro). It'll look like there are twenty different routes and lines because each car is different but, no, there's just one line. They rotate streetcars from all over the world on the line. It costs $6 to ride and exact change is required. Visit Streetcar.org to see which cars are currently out, and to learn about the rest of the fleet.

CABLE CARS

The most iconic form of SF transportation, cable cars were invented in 1873 by Andrew Hallidie, a British man who witnessed a horrible horse accident back in England and thought he could use the hilly landscape in San Francisco to create a safer mode of transport. While twenty-three trolleys were established between 1873 and 1890, only three remain: the Powell-Mason, Powell-Hyde, and California Street lines. It's $6 for a single ride and a lot safer than it looks. While there are faster ways to get around town, a cable car ride is way more fun than a bus. Don't dangle.

OTP Tip: Don't ever get on at Powell and Market. It is like a horde of headless chickens with confused tourists running in every direction. To board from downtown, walk a block or two up to O'Farrell or Geary.

CLIPPER CARDS

A clipper card ($3) is a storage card that encodes all your prepurchased passes and allows you to load cash onto it for circumstances that aren't covered by passes. This makes travel easier, more efficient, and cheaper. For instance, you can load a month of unlimited BART and MUNI rides within SF ($80) and $20 in cash (in case you want to sneak off to Oakland). This will free you from dealing with the add-fare machines inside BART stations and will alleviate the headache of needing exact change for the bus. Check the SFMTA site (or ask an attendant at the Civic Center station) for the passes and discounts that apply to you.

CARS

SF is the city of start-ups, so every carshare

app was either invented here or thrives in its environment. In addition to traditional cabs, you have Uber, Lyft, Freewheel, and InstantCab at your disposal. For rentals, you'll find Zipcar lots everywhere, and FlightCar—like the AirBnB of parked airport cars—operates out of SFO.

BIKES

Bike rental shops are scattered all around the city, and our favorite is City Ride Bikes in Hayes Valley, where they'll rent you less clunky bikes for a fair price. Wait, biking uphill? San Franciscans don't possess superhuman quads that propel them up giant bitch hills with minimal effort. They do the Wiggle, a zigzagging, flat bike path that will get you from Market Street (at Duboce) to Golden Gate Park (via the Haight). The path is a series of left and right turns that take you through some beautiful scenery. You can follow the signs; just make sure to wear a helmet because the fixies go apeshit crazy on there.

FEET

Walking in San Francisco is a workout, but doable. The walk from Fisherman's Wharf down to the Ferry building along the Embarcadero is a popular tourist route that's flat and scenic. Getting from downtown to the Haight and then Golden Gate Park is a bit of a trek. Walking up from the Mission to Noe Valley and over to the Castro can count as your daily cardio workout. Wear your chucks or hop on a bus when things get too vertical.

ACCOMMODATIONS

San Francisco is tiny, and each residential building is densely packed. Many people compromise their living rooms to create another bedroom and will often share a room with a stranger to save on rent. But finding a temporary place to stay is actually not so hard if you're flexible with the arrangements.

HOSTELS

There are a handful of top-notch hostels in San Francisco, and a bunch of really shitty ones (usually in the Tenderloin). Be wary of SRO (single-room occupancy) units; they advertise as hotels but tend to be home-less shelters.

Adelaide Hostel

5 Isadora Duncan Lane
$31–$33, dorms; $89–$159, private

Adelaide is located in a really nice part of the Tenderloin; search for the gorgeous mural to guide the way to the hostel, located deep in an alley. Hippies from all over the world hang outside in their garden patio and the bunk beds here feel like you're on an old train with curtains that you can draw for extra privacy. The décor here is arty and homey, with vintage furniture and quirky touches. They serve free breakfast, throw dinner parties, and put on bar crawls. Everyone here is welcoming and the whole place has a certain vintage charm.

Green Tortoise Hostel

494 Broadway Street
$30–$60, dorms; $85–$90, private

The Green Tortoise is a hippie hostel with an open atrium, a pool table, a fully stocked kitchen, and views of downtown. It's located

in North Beach, right at the bottom of the slope, on the Kearny Street steps, and walk-ing distance from cool bars and restaurants. The place is clean, with laundry on site, and the rooms are well maintained. They put on pub crawls, game nights, and free dinners in the ballroom.

HI International

Fort Mason, Building 240
$30–$42, dorms; $75–$109, private

Upholding the Hostelling International (HI) hostels standard, this location (one of three in the city) is an old military barracks right by Fisherman's Wharf. You'll be elbow to elbow with all the other tourists, but you'll have easy access to the rest of the city. The buildings are situated right on the water with gorgeous views of the bay (and the bridge!) and manicured landscaping all around. There's a café, a big kitchen, and an outdoor deck. This hostel feels like a lodge, with wooden bunks and a fireplace in the common area. The perk of being on federal land is that you never have to pay taxes. The HI downtown location (312 Mason Street) is legit and situated between a liquor store and Café Mason and across the street from Go-Cart tours. The Tenderloin location is shit.

BED-AND-BREAKFASTS AND HOTELS

Bed-and-breakfasts in San Francisco give you a chance to temporarily live inside exquisite architecture. Many homes are old Victorians or Edwardians and come with beautiful bay windows and intricate architectural details.

Dolores Place
3842 25th Street
$139 (plus tax), 3-4 night minimum

A studio in a great location, Dolores Place sits right in Noe Valley, a block from the main 24th Street drag, and a walkable distance from the Mission and the Castro. It features a queen bed, private bath, and a little deck. If you're traveling as a pair, this works out well, as double occupancy is the same rate. It's a little fancier than we're used to, but it makes for a romantic getaway.

Moffatt House Bed & Breakfast
1401 7th Avenue
$84-$114, rooms; $148-$158, suite

It may be located away from the city center in the Inner Sunset, but you'll be right near Golden Gate Park, some excellent cheap restaurants, and the N Judah line that'll get you downtown fast. This B&B is composed of three different rooms, all with windows and a suite on the ground floor with a kitchen, bath, and sitting area. Shoot for room D, which has its own terrace and comfortably accommodates two (but can fit three). The guests here range in age, but it generally attracts older people and families.

IN-LAWS/CRAIGSLIST/AIRBNB

What the fuck's an "in-law"? It's essentially a guesthouse where your in-laws would stay if they came for a visit. Many homes in San Francisco were built with family in mind, and people fortunate enough to own a house will rent out that extra space to temporary visitors. These listings often appear on

Craigslist and AirBnB, are usually in nicer areas (like Pacific Heights, Russian Hill, the Marina, Noe Valley, Bernal Heights, and the Castro), and are priced cheaper per night (or week) than hotel rooms.

COUCHSURFING/CO-OPS

The great thing about this city is that everyone has a crash space for a friend who missed the last BART across the bay, and they'll often put that couch up for rent when it's not in use. To save on rent (and because they're lovable hippies), people will often live in co-op communes, or larger groups of people who share a house. You can get in on all this action via Couchsurfing (or Craigslist).

MONEY

San Francisco is split between pay-with-the-tap-of-tech and cash-only. The Gold Rush happened here, and in many neighborhoods people are still counting coins and scoffing at credit. The most notorious cash-only places are North Beach dive bars, Irish pubs in the Sunset and Richmond districts, Castro bars, and Mission taco places. Since SF has such a thriving food truck culture, having cash on hand to pay for street treats is always a good idea. If you're not planning to buy a clipper card, you must have exact change for the bus ($2.25) and cash when exiting the BART station, just in case. Corner stores usually have a $5–$10 credit card minimum.

HEALTH AND SAFETY

HEALTH

Northern California is one of the healthiest places in the country. You'll find an abundance of organic food, fresh air, and water you can drink from the tap, but as with anywhere, your body may decide to be a jerk anyway. Lucky for you, there are fresh-pressed juice places on every block and over-the-counter meds at drugstores to nurse you back to health.

San Francisco is very sex-positive and should anything funky go down, you have many resources. Planned Parenthood has two Mission locations, a clean clinic at 1650 Valencia Street, and a medical center at 1294 Potrero Avenue. There are community clinics in every neighborhood and over-the-counter morning-after pills are available at drugstores like CVS and Walgreens. AIDS has always been a concern, both medically and politically. Wrap it up, then slap it with a leather whip.

SAFETY

Homeless people are friendlier than your average store clerk, but that doesn't mean there aren't crazies on the streets. You will see some insane things on the MUNI. But drunken old pimps, screaming obscenities with a gold cane in one hand and a Bud Light in the other, are no reason for alarm. People shit on the streets in broad daylight and dress up as fluorescent forest creatures when Halloween is nowhere in sight. This is the norm.

This place is hilly as fuck. We're not going to mother you on how to ride your bike around SF, but bombing down a hill equals a faceplant, which equals a concussion pretty quickly. Keep your ego in check, your brakes well lubed, and wear a helmet.

SF is as lax as it gets about drugs. The quality and availability of marijuana is unparalleled and there's no need to buy it on the street anymore. Go to a clinic, tell them you can't sleep or see, and they'll hook you up with a member card. Dispensaries are everywhere and you can buy top-notch shit, including edibles, for cheap. If you do buy it on the streets, especially near the Haight, you risk getting robbed by a crackhead. As for harder things, the whole city moves to EDM and often with the assistance of Molly and coke. Just about every club and festival has a "guy."

Earthquakes: They happen. What to do? Don't die.

CLIMATE

Northern California is known for fog and the Bay Area attracts the thickest of cloudy murkiness. This means that, even during the peak of summer, the morning starts with a gloomy, humid mess that eventually either burns off into sunny skies or turns to rain.

You'll have to stay flexible and wear layers or change a couple times a day. There are also *microclimates*, a term that refers to how markedly different the weather can be, depending on which neighborhood you're in. For instance, in the Mission, the sun shines much more brightly, since the flat 'hood doesn't collect much fog. Luckily, the winters aren't very harsh. You'll need to bundle up a bit, but it never dips low enough to freeze your snot. Bring a sweatshirt no matter what time of year you're here.

CULTURE AND POLITICS

CULTURE

Food and Drink

San Franciscans are innovators in all matters when it comes to food. Using the wealth of produce available in northern California, chefs across the city focus on local, seasonal, and sustainable food. This city has a close bond with its food history as well, with century-old restaurants like Boudin and Tadich Grill still holding their ground. Known for their sourdough, fresh seafood, and organic produce, San Franciscans savor a range of good food, available here from the street level up to $300 chef's tasting menus. Food entrepreneurship, in the form of food trucks and pop-ups, has always been embraced, and farmers' markets are big productions. The multitude of cultures that inhabit San Francisco make it a master of fusion, from Mexi-Chinese to Franco-Italian to Jap-Korean.

The city's love for food is only equaled by its dedication to booze, and the pairing of the two. Places like Bourbon & Branch, Local Edition, Third Rail, and the Alchemist set the standard for mixologists worldwide. San Francisco bar masters use unheard-of ingredients, extract flavors from unlikely sources, and then blend them to create unique taste profiles. Plus, there's more craft beer here than at a Belgian monastery.

Old-timers like Anchor Brewery are still respected, but newer microbreweries like 21st Amendment and Cellarmaker are popping up everywhere, rethinking brewing methods, turning out amazing seasonal brews, and making eye-catching labels. Then there's wine. You know about Napa, right? If taking a tour of wineries is too rich for your budget, you can pick up a tasty bottle of local wine at a corner store for under $10. Everyone also inexplicably loves to take shots of funky-ass Fernet.

Environment

San Francisco has a thriving environmentalist culture. California has made many advances in the field of conservation and preservation. Plastic bags were banned and it's second nature to bring a spare bag with you wherever you go. Advertisements on public transportation encourage residents to use less water, compost more, and eat less meat and dairy. Nobody dares to litter.

Festivals

Whether they're congregating for music, art, film, food, sex, community development, or a giant mash-up of everything, people in San Francisco love their festivals. You'll find die-hard fest-goers smoking weed, wearing flower wreaths, and sporting booty shorts well into old age. Open-air markets here come with legit DJs, and EDM bumps in the oddest of places (like the California Academy of Sciences). From the free expression of kinky sex at the Folsom Street Fair, to the celebration of Japanese culture at the Cherry Blossom Festival, San Franciscans love to gather in large groups to dance, eat, and sometimes spank each other. Burning Man started here. Enough said.

Entrepreneurship

San Francisco is the start-up epicenter of the world, and entrepreneurship has a huge impact on the city's culture. People find wealth in their twenties, which has the same awkward social implications experienced by a genius who starts college before puberty. Young millionaires don't want to live in single-family homes in the boonies (where they tend to work). They want to party, eat well, own the best gadgets, and reside in the happening spots around town. This creates certain cultural tensions between them and people who actually go to dive bars and eat street food because that's all they can afford.

FUN FACT

Cupertino, the Silicon Valley headquarters of Apple, is the eleventh wealthiest city in the United States.

POLITICS

Gentrification

As a side effect of its entrepreneurial culture, San Francisco is experiencing a big boom in realtor-driven gentrification. As is the case everywhere, when new money comes into a neighborhood, realtors follow to snatch up and develop as much property as possible, stepping over whoever may already live or work there. As a result, many small businesses are bought out and replaced with eyesore condos with units that are astronomically more expensive than a typical resident can afford. This has been the case with small music venues. Cocomo's and Sound Factory already closed their doors and places like the Chapel, Elbo Room, Slim's, and the

Independent are barely hanging on. Gentrification also undermines the preservation of cultural identity in places like the Mission, where Latino-owned businesses are in decline.

Sexuality

Whether you're gay, straight, or somewhere in between, San Francisco's freedom of expression extends to sexuality. The Castro (the largest community of openly gay people in the country) and the Pride Parade here is a huge deal. While the assassination of beloved city supervisor Harvey Milk will forever be ingrained in the collective psyche here, this area continues to make advancements toward equal rights, with openly gay and transgendered people holding high government positions, and the legalization of gay marriage.

Political Awareness

San Francisco has always been a liberal, open-minded place, and residents pride themselves on being up on their politics. Advancements in equal rights for the LGBTQ communities, women, and minorities, and the legalization of medical marijuana, have all been made possible because people here vote, protest, and unionize.

FASHION

San Francisco is Birkenstock-chic, and what people are wearing changes from morning to lunch. You must dress like a transformer. The heavy fog lingers in the morning but turns into sweltering heat by noon, which means you'll need to layer and peel on the go. People often wear billowy fabrics over their intended outfits to keep the moisture away, with a thin layer that'll easily fit into a bag come midday.

Each neighborhood has its own microclimate and microfashion to match. Downtown it's all business; Nob Hill, Russian Hill, Hayes Valley, and Noe Valley are sprinkled with spa moms in yoga pants; SOMA is all about design and buttoned-up hipster; the Mission is eclectic, with some stuck-in-the-'90s fashions making their way on the streets; the Castro runs wild and many men choose to forgo the confines of clothing altogether; and the Haight burns strong with that hippie look that seems to never get old.

San Franciscans are into working out, and many people wear their spandex throughout the day. People here ride bikes, and often fashion meets function on this front as well; one-leg pant rolls for all.

Nighttime fashion is mostly daywear with glitter, and unless you're a mountain goat, going up the side of steep hills in flashy footwear will be a bitch. Until you figure out the transportation system, commit to chucks.

When it comes to festival-wear, anything goes, no matter how little function it serves, as long as it's utterly absurd.

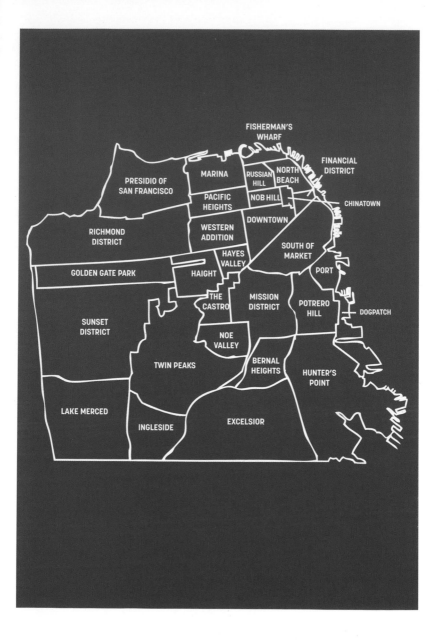

NEIGHBORHOODS

Like a bag of brightly colored jelly beans, San Francisco is filled with little pockets of flavor. For a place that's about the same size as Disneyland, it's surprising that even locals admit to stumbling upon new things after years of living in this dense city. Be it a hidden overlook, an elaborate Chicano mural, historical saloons from the Gold Rush era, or an underground dinner party, there is so much here that it's impossible to see it all. But that's the beauty of it. San Francisco hides things from you among its thick fog and rolling hills. Its neighborhoods are dictated by the landscape and every single one is unique, with its own microclimate, favored mode of transportation, and set of colorful personalities.

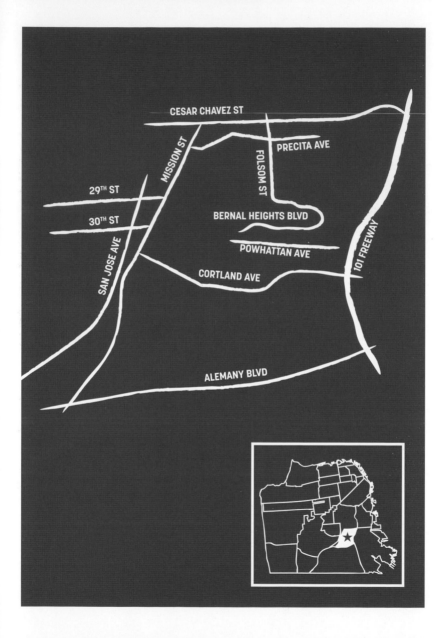

BERNAL HEIGHTS

A serpentine neighborhood around an amazing lookout hill, Bernal Heights is a homey getaway from the Mission madness. Dotted with colorful houses and gorgeous views at every turn, half of this hood sits high up on a hill serviced by the 67 bus. After hitting some of the best bakeries and ice cream shops that hover here, Bernal Park is a perfect hike to revive you from the sugar coma. Down by the freeway, the Alemany Market springs up every weekend and features the largest selection of California produce on Saturdays and a spectacular display of thrifty junk on Sundays.

COFFEE AND BAKERIES

CAFE ST. JORGE
#Portuguese #OptionsForAll
3438 Mission Street

St. Jorge draws an eclectic crowd, from the day workers who take over the outside seating in the morning, to the lunch and laptop crowd. They serve Stumptown and have fantastic breakfast options. St. Jorge stacks their waffles high with fruit, serves quinoa bowls with nuts and a touch of cinnamon, and piles gloriously creamy avocado and fresh figs onto thick-cut toast. Intermingled throughout their menu and décor, you'll find Portuguese touches, namely the flag over the front door and natas (Portuguese egg custards) on the counter. Their walls are neatly decorated with local photographs, there's a makeout window out front with a throw pillow–covered sill, and the little counter is packed with all kinds of surprises, including wine and beer.

LITTLE BEE BAKING
#PastriesFromHeaven #FourBarrelCoffee
#ThreeTwinsIceCream
521 Cortland Avenue

At first you'll see a little hand-painted bee sign right outside, then the shiny tops of the tarts will draw you in further with glistening chocolate panache sitting under the display. From the flaky-topped flourless chocolate brownie and mini-cakes outfitted in muffin papers, to their lightly browned almond macaroons and the salted caramel buttercream on their cupcakes, Little Bee is a simple place with complex flavors. The décor is cottage-chic with just one thin table and a matching wooden church pew near

a little window. This place also takes "local" to a whole new level by posting signs that ask neighbors for their homegrown lemons in exchange for cash or trade.

MITCHELL'S ICE CREAM
#LegendaryIceCream #AsianFlavors
688 San Jose Avenue

Mitchell's makes small batches of wild flavors daily, many with a Southeast Asian flair. The ube, a bright purple yam from the

Philippines, is the way to go big, and ube-macapuno (same yam with coconut chunks mixed in) is the way to go biggest. They've been churning this stuff out since the '50s, and the shop still has that comforting, after-school vibe.

PROGRESSIVE GROUNDS
#AmazingPatio #comfortable
400 Cortland Avenue

The coffee and food here is forgettable, but the space is what'll bring you back for more. The shop feels like coming home to a warm, worn-in house in the hills, complete with a growing garden patio out back and multilevel seating. You can lounge here for hours with your mediocre bagel, and the service is friendly in that neighborly way. There's also a Mission location with the same okay coffee but without all the comforts of home.

SANDBOX BAKERY
#coffee #MorningBun #JapaneseFusion
833 Cortland Avenue

Sandbox distributes all around San Francisco, but going straight to the source brings you closer to the fresh-baked, buttery croissants Frenchmen fantasize about. Made by Mutsumi Takehara, the former pastry chef of several fine-dining kitchens in the city, the items offered are petite and sort of French, with an occasional nod to her Japanese heritage. Sometimes a little yuzu sneaks into the sweet pastries and a bit of miso into the savory. Tiny muffins, gingersnap cookies, macaroons, meat-stuffed brioche, curry-filled challah, and Tartine-worthy morning buns fill the shop. No matter what this woman is baking, you will want to chipmunk it all into your cheeks until you can't breathe.

 # EAT

331 CORTLAND MARKETPLACE
#pierogies #pickles #waffles #RiceBalls
331 Cortland Avenue

Like a coworking space for food vendors, this marketplace is a collection of food stands and caterers in one open storefront. Each holds a yearly renewable lease, where they can just quit at the end or funnel their profits from the marketplace to open their own spot. Walking in here you'll be hit in the face by every smell you can imagine—pickles, freshly baked waffles, Thai spices, and pierogies. Everyone is just happy to be in business doing what they love. You can grab a warm, meaty piroshok from Anda Piroshki, a better-for-you treat from Wholesome Bakery, a worse-for-you-waffle from Suite Food Waffles, and delicious curries and rice balls from Mau Cruna. Paulie's Pickling has been here longest and runs the show; they'll be able to answer all your questions.

EL GRAN TACO LOCO
#BurritosMojados #LateNight
3306 Mission Street

This place is straight up loco. There's a poster of an anthropomorphized taco being chased by a gun-slinging jalapeño at the front entrance, so you know this shit will be crazy good for a drunk stumble-and-chomp. If you don't mind getting messy, the Burrito Loco Mojado Super is a giant wet log of Mexican wonder. Douse it with their spicy salsas at the bar and you've got yourself a Grade A, regret-it-later meal. This isn't the cheapest late-night Mexican joint, but there are no lines at 1 a.m., the food isn't gringo-fied, and their mural is just unlike anywhere else.

EMMY'S SPAGHETTI SHACK
#HomeCookin' #LowRiderDécor
#SpaghettiAndMeatballs
18 Virginia Avenue or 3230 Mission Street

A neighborhood favorite, Emmy's feeds people what they need: a large plate of spaghetti and meatballs that'll require you to lean deep into a grandmother's bosom upon completion for a nap. From the outside, the shack is colorful and quirky, with murals reminiscent of the low-rider era. The menu is a handwritten collection of scribbles and, aside from the fantastic spaghetti, Emmy's lovingly serves ceviche, salads, pasta, a few meat and fish dishes, and inventive cocktails (like the Ryan Gosling; you know you want to, girl). Their newer location on Mission Street serves the same carbs of love with a whatever's clever attitude and more elbow room.

HILLSIDE SUPPER CLUB
#AvoidBrunchLines #TreatYourself
#dinner
300 Precita Avenue

There's this popular, expensive restaurant called Blue Plate a few blocks away on Mission Street, and while their food is on point, brunch wait times will make you cry. The Hillside Supper Club will take your money right away and turn it into edible gold. Tucked into a cozy corner by Folsom Street, this is a quiet spot for a quiet brunch. They serve a savory bread pudding ($13) that's a balance of salty flavors imparted by bacon and white cheddar and comes topped with a sunny-side-up egg. The prices jump up some during dinner ($20–$30 entrées), but the guys behind the Supper Club really

bring out their big guns to showcase their culinary aptitude with dishes that capture their collective influences.

LA SANTANECA
#pupusas #horchata
3781 Mission Street

Since the closing of famed El Zocalo in 2014, La Santaneca is taking over the pupusa party. Their menu features a range of traditional Salvadoran food, but their pupusas, at $1.75 each, steal the show. Those are meat, cheese, and/or bean-stuffed fried rounds; get two of these filling savory cakes and you're done, son. Our go-to is the slightly spicy jalapeño and queso dipped into the remainder of the free salsa you get with chips just for being there. Top it off with some sweet, cinnamony, brown-like-it-should-be horchata and you're set.

LITTLE NEPAL
#momos #HilltopHimalayan
925 Cortland Avenue

If you've never had Nepalese food before, you'll recognize it as a little Indian and a bit Chinese, but with its own distinctive flavors. Little Nepal is a great place to try out this dynamic cuisine for the first time, and its location high up the hill draws some parallels to the geography of the country from which the menu hails. They've got all the staples, like momos (Nepalese dumplings), curries, and well-made noodle dishes to ease you into taste exploration. This may not be the Himalayas, but you'll feel the air thin when you dip into their pungent sauces or wrap your mouth around the Kukhurako Ledo (tender chicken straight from the tandoori). With Bernal Hill right outside, you can climb to the top and almost feel like you've scaled Everest.

NEW BOSWORTH MARKET
#CornerStore #pupusas
145 Bosworth Street

An unassuming corner store that sells all those odds and ends you may need, plus pupusas. There's a little area in the back where you can consume these fresh, handmade Salvadoran snacks with a little lady pumping them out to order. Wait time can get ridiculous, but you have to forgive her; she has tiny hands and once you get yours all warm and cheesy, you won't have a care in the world. These things cost only $1.50 a pop, and you can stock up on TP while you wait.

NOETECA
#brunch #CroqueJosephine
1551 Dolores Street

Noeteca does some naughty things to their brunch sandwiches, like the Croque Josephine. Some people make sandwiches with bread; Noeteca opts for thick slices of savory bread pudding, jammed-up with smoky Black Forest ham, drizzled with some kind of unicorn cheese sauce with a sunny-side egg on top. Other notable dishes are their salmon

tarte flambé (which is like an über-French version of a bagel with lox) and perfectly balanced salads. There will be a lot of couples here getting cozy near the windows. Ignore them and focus on your naughty sandwich.

RED HILL STATION
#seafood #hyperlocal
803 Cortland Avenue

You don't come to California to eat land creatures the whole time. Dive into the deep with this sleek, casual seafood spot. Start off right with a few oysters on the half shell ($2.50 each) and proceed to things with fins. The menu changes frequently but will always feature a simply prepared local fish dish and several variations of linguini. The food is a bit fancy, but not fussy. Follow them on Facebook to see what's cookin'.

OTP Tip: Get the calamari whenever it's on the menu. They go out to Monterey and pull them fresh from the water.

THE FRONT PORCH
#SouthernComfort #MacAndCheese
#FriedChicken
65 29th Street

As much as Guy Fieri annoys the piss out of us, his show's producers do know where to go for down-and-dirty good food. Guy won't go near a place unless it guarantees at least one clogged artery, and Front Porch delivers with bubbly mac and cheese, creamy grits, crispy fried chicken (which you can get on a jalapeño-bacon waffle during brunch), tangy fried pickles, and collard greens. With dishes like the Stoner Stack and the Hangover Helper, the Front Porch won't let you leave without stuffing you full of Southern food that cures whatever ails you.

◉ SEE AND DO

BERNAL HEIGHTS PARK
#UniqueViews #HillsideMansions

There are many places where you can get a view of the city, but the hill at Bernal is something special. You can access the hike several ways: Take the 67 bus to its base and just walk straight up, or hike it up from the Cortland Strip, starting at Anderson Street, and zigzag through the hillside mansions until you find your way to the open park. Once there, you'll wonder how the off-leash dogs don't fly straight off the side of it (gravity's grip at its best). At the top, you'll see a panoramic view of the city with a zoom on downtown if you walk around behind the dilapidated structure. People come up here to read, think, and sometimes set up easels to paint the gorgeous views. The funnest way to climb down from the top is via the public stairs nestled near the homes right by the park's entrance. Don't be a creep and stop to stare into their windows.

Thrills on Billy Goat Hill

Nearby Glen Park hides one of San Francisco's unique treasures. Billy Goat Hill is nothing but a patch of green with a large tree up some rickety stairs on Thirtieth and Beacon Streets. Once you get up there, you'll see a completely unsafe swing dangling from the tree's branches. Your gut will tell you that this is how people fall off mountains to their death, but ignore your insides and hop on. Once your dangling feet swing out into the aerial city view, you will be overtaken by childlike joy. Keep your lunch down and set your spirit free.

THE NEW WHEEL ELECTRIC BIKES

#PowerToYourPedal #BikeRentals
420 Cortland Avenue

This bike shop is different, starting with the crescent bike rack out front. They carry electric bicycles that are perfect for the SF landscape. New Wheel makes it possible to ride through everything that may otherwise interrupt your ride, by stocking bikes that work with your pedaling to assist you as you go uphill. It's $85 a day (helmet, maps, lock, and bag included) to rent an ebike, with a $25 refundable deposit and an option to buy the bike if you fall in love after two days (where the $170 you paid for a two-day rental can be applied to the purchase price). It's more expensive than renting a traditional bike, but will help you cover much more ground.

WILLIE NELSON WINDOW

#WillieNelsonForPresident
Cortland and Bennington Streets

Half a block up from Cortland on Bennington, you'll see a window dedicated to Willie Nelson. It's packed with mugs and knick-knacks collected and displayed in the man's honor. There's also a poster on the door urging you to vote for Willie Nelson for president (in 2012). We don't know what drives someone to create a Willie Nelson shrine, but this is the kind of quirk that keeps San Francisco so charmingly weird.

🏪 SHOP

by the variety of produce available here. Alemany's mostly Mexican and Chinese vendors sell spiny melons, Thai chili bushes ($1 each), rambutans, and pea greens, in addition to more common produce. Here, you'd have a hard time spending $20 for a week's worth of groceries. If you come when they start packing up (1:30 p.m.), vendors will unload their goods for $1 (huge bags of tomatoes, fruit, etc.), and sometimes give it away for free. Prepared food stalls line the perimeter, including All Star Tamales, which live up to their name with a huge variety of prepared-to-order tamales ($3.25 each) wrapped in corn leaves. Little picnic tables are tucked between the vendors so you can sit and enjoy your market finds with the subtle rush of the freeway in your periph.

OTP Tip: The flea market that takes place here on Sundays feels like a secret gun market, but is full of actual flea stuff (and not expensive artisan goods) like silver, leather, Grandma's figurines, cassettes, beat-up furniture, and other attic junk.

ALEMANY MARKET

#UniqueProduce #WeekendFun #cheap
100 Alemany Boulevard

Among the many farmers' markets in the city, this one stands out, despite being dangerously close to the noisy 101 freeway. Stretching as far as the eye can see, you'll find several rows of vendors tucked into concrete structures. As you make your way down the stands, you'll be blown away

HILLWIDE GARAGE SALE

#JunkHunt #UniqueSouvenirs

Every August, the entire hillside neighborhood organizes a collective purge of stuff by registering for the Hillwide Garage Sale. You can bounce between front lawns and haggle your way into one-of-a-kind finds. A fun way to see the neighborhood and meet some interesting residents, hitting the garage sale is also a unique approach to souvenir shopping. The sale raises money for the Bernal Hill Neighborhood Center and draws about five thousand visitors every year.

PARTYING

EL RIO
#dive #games #DaytimeDanceParty
3158 Mission Street

On any given night, El Rio is just pure fun encased in a well-stocked bar with an expansive backyard, complete with a ping-pong table and performance stage. Mondays are all about $1 Tecates during happy hour and funky hip-hop tunes. The music gets eclectic on Tuesdays with random performances in the yard, most for free. Wednesdays will lure you to sing off-pitch karaoke, Thursdays test your ping-pong skills at 5 p.m., and Fridays get freaky with burlesque. The first Saturday of every month is "Hard French," a daytime (mostly gay) dance party where everyone ends up honoring the name of the event with sloppy makeout sessions.

HOLY WATER
#HolyCocktails #ghostly
309 Cortland Avenue

A sexy bar with raised black tables, an eerie baptism mural on the wall, and ghostly holy bottles painted above the front window outside, Holy Water sets the mood for cocktails, and for $9 each you'll want to dip into several. The refreshing cucumber Holy Gimlet, the After the Gold Rush, and punchy Mexican Firing Squad (with deep-flavored reposado) will start you on your holy journey. Sip your drinks slowly and make sure to stay alert for the eleventh hour (11 p.m.) when the bar starts pouring interesting craft beers, specialty experimental cocktails, and you can play "Bartender's Choice" when you pick two ingredients and watch them craft something tasty.

IRON & GOLD
#Speakeasyesque #cocktails
3187 Mission Street

Iron & Gold is not really a speakeasy, but puts out that vibe with its "so dim it's almost pitch-black" lighting. Come here when you have a massive zit and still need to socialize, or on a cold night to crouch by the fireplace with a Hot Toddy ($7). Their cocktails are strong and a bit cheaper than most places. The Joaquin Murrieta stirred our curiosity because it comes with an interesting backstory of a man whose cut-off head was stuck in a jar of alcohol. The drink itself was delicious, tequila-based with chocolate and orange bitters, and a cherry floating on top to really put the nail in the coffin.

KNOCKOUT

#dance #bingo #ThemedNights
#BootyBasement
3223 Mission Street

The KO is dancing on the edge of douchey. They throw some wild parties and the turnout is usually one or two bros away from the dumps, but surprisingly it never reaches critical ass mass. Their Thursday bingo nights are perfect when you want to play old-people games among a drunk and rowdy crowd, and their monthly $5 Booty Basement parties (third Saturdays) are a guaranteed sweaty good time.

ROCK BAR

#local #NicerThanADive #MeatCocktails
80 29th Street

A local mining-themed bar, covered in actual rocks on the outside with quirky dive touches once you step indoors. They've got a long list of house cocktails, some that feature meat, and a Bloody Mary that might as well be a salad. A great Monday spot, since their happy hour runs all day, the Rock Bar also has a shabby vanity in the bathroom so you can watch your face go from polished to plastered.

WILD SIDE WEST

#dive #backyard #BernalHeights
424 Cortland Avenue

Wild Side West is a big part of SF's gay history, as it was one of the first lesbian bars. The sculptures out back (and some of the art on the walls) are old items antigay protesters tossed in front of the bar, which the owners turned into art instead of hate. Lots of lesbians come here to make out and you should, too. Here's the game plan: Squeeze up to the bar, get a cheap beer ($2 PBRs),

then do whatever it takes to push through to the backyard. It's a magical place covered in plants, with nooks and benches all around, birds singing during the day, and saliva-swapping sounds at night.

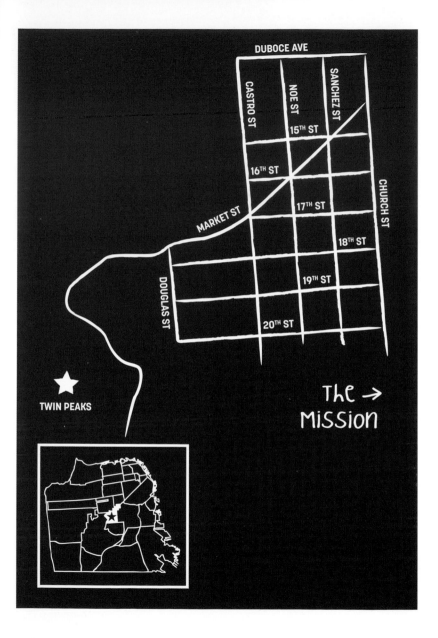

CASTRO/ DUBOCE

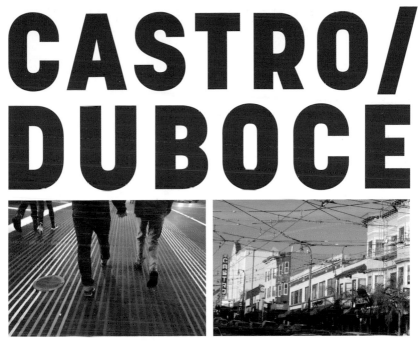

In the Castro, guys will feel like the prettiest girl in the room and girls will feel like they need to work on their personalities to get attention. Regardless of your sexuality, the Castro is a great place to get one with gay. This isn't the neighborhood embodiment of that one flamboyant gay friend, but a historic neighborhood where people are proud to be out and a place that has influenced progressive movements around the nation. From the rainbow-painted crosswalks to the giant flag that flies over Market and Castro Streets, the Castro further plays up its gay with bakeries that sell dick cookies, glittery window displays, and the most fabulous drag queens in the world. Will you see completely naked men on the streets in broad daylight? Yeah, so?

☕ COFFEE AND BAKERIES

CAFÉ UB
#GoodWiFi #RitualCoffee
3901 18th Street

Nothing fancy, UB is a little spot serving Ritual coffee and homemade empanadas with a hearty side of WiFi. The pace of this place is on the slower side, so once you get your caffeine hit, things will be moving at a snail's pace. It's a good spot to grab a bagel and a latte and get some people-watching done through the window early in the morning.

ESPRESSAMENTE ILLY
#FamousCoffee #BigCupWindow
2349 Market Street

Illy is a brand with a long history that dates back to 1933, when a Hungarian (Francesco Illy) fell in love with coffee upon visiting Trieste, Italy. He made it his life's mission to innovate the business of coffee production. The Castro outpost of Espressamente Illy features a giant espresso cup in the front window and sculptures made out of a bunch of little cups scattered about and woven into the light fixtures. Everything in here is red and white, except for the coffee, which is brown and delicious.

FIVE STAR TRUFFLES
#chocolate #IceCream
4251A 18th Street

Five Star is just a hole in the wall with bins of truffles. You never see anybody hanging out in here, so we've come to the conclusion that people run in wide-eyed and secretly shove a bunch of truffles in their face before nonchalantly returning to the sidewalk. These things are so rich and creamy and the coconut flavor, while tiny, tastes like you've consumed an entire island nation. Plus, they serve ice cream and you get a free truffle with your purchase.

HOT COOKIE
#DickCookies #DicksOnSticks
407 Castro Street

Just when you thought you've tried every kind of cookie, a place like Hot Cookie adds dick cookies to the mix—giant, chocolate-covered, phallic cookies that are perfectly fitting for the Castro. When food is based on gimmicks, quality usually suffers, but these $6 dicks actually taste good (like coconut macaroons) and you can get them skewered through the balls on a stick for easy handling. They also bake more traditionally shaped cookies (in fun flavors like toffee and macadamia nut) that are sold by weight, but when dick cookies are on the table, nobody cares about anything else.

REVEILLE COFFEE
#GreatAtmosphere #DesignOriented
4076 18th Street

With several locations around the city (and a truck in FiDi), this café is top-notch when it

comes to design. The inspired décor consists of a wood-log wall, a counter wrapped in black-and-white print, tastefully selected chairs (mod leather loungers), an open-front patio with benches, and one phallic cactus on the shelf for that Castro flair. The coffee is strong and luscious, the pastries are thoughtfully crafted, the food is on the fancier side (like quinoa salad, various flatbreads, and sandwiches), and the barista is so nice you'll want to tip him twice.

SPIKE'S COFFEES & TEAS
#NoWiFi #BulldogCups
4117 19th Street

Bulldogs are popular in the Castro and you'll see Spike's printed dog traveling on many a cup. Spike's is all about promoting conversation in the community, so you won't find WiFi here, just a bunch of people hyped up on indie coffee, sprawled out on the outdoor patio discussing the haps. The shop is filled with jars of cookies, candy, and brownies,

with croissants and other baked goods under glass below. They really care about latte art and they have fantastic tea (like the Russian Caravan or Cinnamon Orangerie). This shop is a little old, a little new, with a crowd to match.

THOROUGH BREAD & PASTRY
#TinyPastries #BreadPudding #backyard
248 Church Street

This place is a little awkward in a lot of ways, but their excellent bread and pastries make it all okay. They make sandwiches with their own fresh-baked bread, and while the baked goods are smaller than average, they're dense and packed with flavor. Beautifully displayed under the glass counter up front, you'll find fancy little personal cakes, tarts, three-bite cheese Danishes, and microscopic cream puffs. The only thing they go big on is their sweet or savory bread pudding, served in a huge square chunk. Don't make the mistake of sitting inside or up front; the backyard has swaying trees and chirping birds.

 **EAT**

ANCHOR OYSTER BAR
#FreshOysters #cioppino #TreatYourself
579 Castro Street

This place is small, but the mirrored back makes it look a lot bigger, and once inside, you'll feel like you're on a boat. This one is going to cost you, but Anchor serves some of the best seafood in San Francisco. A good way to sample everything Anchor's got to offer is their special, where you get twelve oysters, eight steamed clams, and four grilled prawns for $39.95. Split that with a friend to keep the cost down. Anchor's cioppino ($33.95 for a small, but big enough for two) is packed with every shelled, finned, and clawed creature you can imagine in a savory, acidic broth. The wait is usually long, but that will give you time to convince yourself that parting with $40 for a plate of seafood is a good idea.

BISOU
#BottomlessBrunch #benedicts
2367 Market Street

Any place that goes bottomless gets packed for weekend brunch. Bisou does $20 bottom-

less mimosas (or Bloody Marys) and has an entire menu section dedicated to just egg benedicts. The best variation is the Pork Belly Benedict (with beef cheeks in close second), which comes with a truffled hollandaise that brings the salty smokiness of the pork to a new, earthy level. The best seat in the house is on the upper balcony, where you can watch people go from sleepy to sloshed.

CAFÉ FLORE
#OutdoorParadise
#PeopleWatchingWindows
2298 Market Street

Eating at Café Flore is like sitting down in a faraway garden with a bunch of hot guys and their dogs. There are gorgeous plants everywhere in the spacious outdoor patio, and the inside is all wrapped in windows that create an enjoyable, almost outdoors ambience. Come for a morning avocado toast topped with a runny egg ($5.50) or a light lunch salad. Café Flore is a breath of fresh air despite the fumes wafting off this busy corner of Market and Castro Streets.

EIJI
#FreshTofu #sashimi #mochi
317 Sanchez Street

The big deal here is a jiggly bowl of tofu. Sounds delicious, right? Hear us out: The oboro is a bowl of pure white, creamy tofu freshly made to order that comes with pods of accoutrements (like shiso, grated ginger, scallions, bonito flakes, sesame seeds, and spicy radish) that you add to each bite for a new adventure every time. Also, the fish here is so fresh that you'll want to avoid mucking it up with rice, soy sauce, or anything else. To finish, the fresh strawberry mochi is an entire strawberry encased in sweet, floury dough. The place might be small, but bring a big appetite.

EL CASTILLITO
#HugePortions #SuperBurritos
136 Church Street

El Castillito serves a gigantic super burrito that isn't just stuffed with sour cream, guac, and cheese, but also takes on a hulklike quality, growing into an edible torpedo of bowl-breaking proportions. The Al Pastor, sweet, succulent pork with onions doused in their salsas, is your entry into the Mexican gates of heaven (and will cost you well below $10). Check out the murals on the walls if you can see through your tears of joy.

GYRO XPRESS
#falafel #QuickLunch
499 Castro Street

With a name like Gyro Xpress and the fact that it looks like a shitty chain, you'd think twice about eating here. But you'd be missing out on some of the biggest, crunchiest falafel you've ever had. This place serves seriously large falafel that come four per combo plate ($9.95) with sesame-sprinkled exteriors. The hummus is spot-on, the tabletop hot sauce is amazing, the yogurt tzatziki has herbaceous dill flavor with a kick, and the freshly made pitas come to you warm and fluffy. It may not look like much from the outside and the service can be spotty, but it's seriously delicious.

it whateverthefuck he wants. For instance, the Menage à Trois is loaded with BBQ sauce, chicken, cheddar, pepper jack, Swiss, honey mustard, and actual honey (get it with extra dirty sauce to complete the pun). Ike's is perfect for vegans, those with more animalistic tendencies, and just about anyone with a mouth and a sense of humor.

FUN FACT

Dutch Crunch is the secret bread that everyone in the Bay Area knows and nobody else has ever heard of. Except for the Netherlanders, who call it "Tiger Bread" for its crackly top.

IKE'S PLACE
#CrazySandwiches #SecretDirtySauce #DutchCrunch
3489 16th Street

Even glu-tards will risk their lives to taste what the Ike is cookin' (there's a gluten-free menu, don't go dying). The undisputed king of sandwiches, Ike's milelong menu doesn't have a dud in the bunch. Ike puts crazy shit between freshly baked bread (giraffe-patterned Dutch Crunch is a must), spreading on his secret dirty sauce, and then naming

L'ARDOISE BISTRO
#Duboce #TreatYourself #romantic
151 Noe Street

This romantic French bistro has a whole luxurious sidewalk park with plants and benches up front. The atmosphere is white tablecloth, wineglass chic. We're suckers for Coq au Vin and theirs is spectacular, fall-off-the-bone tender, and has deep, slow-cooked wine flavor. While the prices are up there, the portions are bigger than your average fine-dining place and the atmosphere is so sexy that you'll effectively replace your hungry with horny by the end of the meal.

MAMA JI'S
#DimSum #Sichuan
4416 18th Street

When there are several vibrant Chinatowns within arm's reach, why would anybody venture into the Castro for dim sum or

Sichuan? MaMa Ji's is great because sometimes you're just not all there to figure out Chinese and this spot caters to good ol' Americans without sacrificing authenticity or quality. Not convinced? Try the chili-loaded Hot and Numbing Fish and once your mouth stops burning, we can talk. As far as dim sum is concerned, MaMa's got all the goods: dumplings, buns, and shumai. The prices are fair, the service is kind, the space is inviting, and they serve Belgian beers.

ORPHAN ANDY'S
#DrunkFood #24Hours
3991 17th Street

Come here when you've had a few and get the sudden urge for pancakes at 2 a.m. The service will suck (these people work all night, what can you expect?), there will be a bunch of screaming, half-naked dudes, and things will be far from refined. But you will get your pancakes ($7 for two) and maybe

some bacon, and well, fuck it—OJ, too—because breakfast starts whenever you feel like it.

SLURP NOODLE BAR
#AsianFusion #ramen
469 Castro Street

A casual place to slurp down some noodles with outdoor seating up front so everyone can see the broth hit your nose. A new addition to the hood, Slurp is Asian fusion and the slurpiest item on their menu is pork belly ramen. They also serve things to bite, like pork buns and papaya salad, but you can make the slurping sound anyway if you're feeling particularly obnoxious.

STARBELLY
#brunch #EggPizza
3583 16th Street

The same people who own this place also own popular fancypants Beretta down in the Mission, and during dinnertime it plays up to a chic crowd. Brunch is a different story here; it's all about thin-crust pizzas ($15) with crispy chorizo and runny sunny-side-up eggs. While they could pay the rent with pizzas alone, they also feature dishes with Prather Ranch beef, like the loco moco ($11), a meat patty with rice, eggs, and soy; and a big-ass burger ($11), to which you could (and absolutely should) add Point Reyes blue cheese (for $2 more). A perk of eating brunch at a fancy dinner place is that the wine selection is carried over from the nighttime wino crowd.

◉ SEE AND DO

CASTRO THEATRE
#SingAlongs #FilmFestivals
#OldMoviesIn3D
429 Castro Street

The décor will absolutely blow you away with its ornate chapel ceiling, balconies, and golden walls. There is a big organ that sits right in the middle of the stage where a guy plays lots of show tunes while everybody gets seated and during intermissions. This thing looks like a spaceship flight control room and lowers into the ground once he's done piping its pipes. The theater is a huge, open, regal space with old pictures of SF celebrities and scenes on the screen before the show instead of those shitty commercials you see elsewhere. The theater does double features, sometimes in 3D (we saw *Jaws*; it was awesome) and patrons are encouraged to talk shit about the movie while it's playing. They hold full-on sing-alongs and drag shows, which turns it into more of a social event and not just a movie theater.

FUN FACT

Peaches Christ and Heklina are the most decorated and celebrated queens of the Castro. Find them at political events, late-night parties, or walking the streets in all their glittery glory.

SEWARD STREET SLIDES
#slides #FindYourInnerKidAgain
Intersection of Douglas and Seward Streets

On a hill, where Douglas and Seward Streets meet, you will find a duo of concrete slides, usually with no kids in sight. Haul up a piece of cardboard (unless you want ass burn) and hang onto it as you slide way down the street. This isn't Six Flags caliber, but it's no kiddie slide, either; you will get at least one butterfly in your stomach on the way down. They get busy with curious tourists on weekends and are boarded up at 5 p.m. daily.

TWIN PEAKS
#PanoramicViews #KickAssHike

The Twin Peaks are the highest points in San Francisco. Leave your phone at home and don't get step-by-step directions; just walk up 24th Street from the BART station until the peaks appear and figure out how to get up there. (Hint: Many public staircases are tucked around houses, including a swirly one over Market Street.) You'll have two peaks to hike once you get up there, with rickety stairs around the base of the ascent. At the top of the peaks you'll find 360-degree views of SF, a close-up of the Sutro Tower, and some terrifying self-cleaning toilets. No matter the time of year, it gets very windy

and cold up there. Bring a hoodie and a hand-held lunch.

OTP Tip: For the lazy approach, take the 37 bus all the way up to the base of the hike.

🏪 SHOP

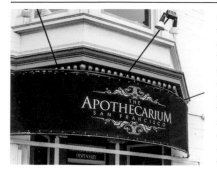

APOTHECARIUM
#CannabisDispensary #FancyAsFuck
2095 Market Street

Like stepping into a French boutique with wall sconces, lace-patterned walls, and chic furniture, the Apothecarium is by far the fanciest place to get your "medical" marijuana. Their edibles, like brownies, cookies, and bars, look like something out of a pastry kitchen and nothing like those sad bricks of dough and weed available elsewhere. They boast a curated bud menu (averaging $15 per gram) and will explain each individual plant's characteristics thoroughly. For those who already got too high on their own supply, the Apothecarium also delivers to their members for a $10 fee.

CLIFF'S VARIETY STORE
#hardware #toys #DragSupplies
#CoolWindowDisplay
479 Castro Street

A historic variety store that's split into two sides, each with an amazing front display window that usually showcases mechanical muppet trannies. The main store carries hardware but with flair (like colorful hammers), in addition to costume accessories and masks, toys, rainbow flag gear, screwdriver pens, garden gnomes, board games, crafts, and cooking supplies. The smaller side store has gifts like "dirty bitch soap," feathers, boas, fabric, patches, glitter, inventive bathroom stuff, and a large selection of loofahs. You'll come in to aimlessly browse and leave with a bag full of beads, feathers, and a rainbow crescent wrench.

CROSSROADS
#SecondHandFinds #BestOfTheChain
2123 Market Street

This nationwide secondhand store started in San Francisco in 1991 and their Castro location has the best selection by far. Here, you'll find a wide array of shoes, mid-level designer dresses, and brands like Free People, with about 30 percent of the inventory fluffed up by H&M and Forever 21. Since this area is gay man paradise, the men's section is fantastic, with Levis, button-downs, T-shirts, fashionable cardigans, and boat shoes. After you check your bag at the counter, the staff leaves you the fuck alone so you can dig for days in this well-organized store.

PARTYING

440 CASTRO
440 Castro Street

Sometimes people will refer to 440 as "Daddy's" because it's a notorious hangout for older rich guys. If this sounds like you, come here to pick up your young, doe-eyed counterpart. If the hair on your chest hasn't quite grown in, this place has two-for-one drink specials, $3 margaritas, and an *Addams Family* pinball machine. As if everyone isn't hitting on each other enough already, on Mondays the boys strip down to their skimpies for Underwear Night, which sometimes ends in a battle of the bulge.

OTP Tip: If you get hungry, take your daddy to Thailand Restaurant right next door. You will have to climb up some shifty stairs, as if you're going into someone's apartment, but you'll then step into a no-frills Thai restaurant with a view of the Castro Theatre.

BADLANDS
#WhenAllYouWantToDoIsDance
#2For1HappyHour
4121 18th Street

Badlands is the perfect caricature of a stereotypical gay club, but in the best way. No matter who or what you're into, Badlands opens its big bad arms and welcomes you to dance to Madonna, old Britney, and classic disco, all backed by music videos on the projector. The drinks are cheap ($6 cocktails) and stiff, which more than makes up for the small cover ($3–$5). Come rev the dance engine during their twofer happy hour, from 3 to 8 p.m., Monday to Saturday, and get into something strange before the night is over.

BEAUX
#lounge #CheerfulBartenders
#DanceParties
2344 Market Street

During the day, this place looks like a bank lobby, but we assure you it gets crazy on the weekends. It's a relative newcomer to the scene. Start early so you can cozy up on the orange-leather lounge chairs and get to know the notoriously cheerful bartenders. If you're here on Manimal Fridays (where drinks are $2 between 8:30 and 10 p.m. and there's no cover), prepare for practically naked go-go dancers and mostly electronic beats. Ladies, Beaux hasn't forgotten about you; every Thursday is all about the Pussy Party, a happy hour for ladies from 4 to 9 p.m., with two-for-one drinks and $1 pink pussy shots.

BLACKBIRD
#CocktailLounge #Duboce
2124 Market Street

Blackbird does cocktails well with only a speck of pretension in the air. During their weekday happy hours (5 to 8 p.m.), the "savvy spender" can "drink like a horse for the price of a bird," and, well, cocktails are only $4.

CHURCHILL
#Duboce #cocktails
198 Church Street

The place has a dungeonlike (sexy not rapey) vibe, with ropes on the ceilings, plush couches, storm cellar-like lights, and black drapes over the windows. This is the kind of place where you'll want to drink Bulleit, and lucky for you they've got a cocktail that'll hit the spot called the Jennie Jerome from Brooklyn. Nobody likes gin, but Churchill makes it a notch better with their version of the classic Aviation cocktail (served in a mason jar). Their featured cocktails change regularly, but are consistently great and average around $9.

HI TOPS
#JockstrapShots #WingsOnMondays
2247 Market Street

Hi Tops's Gym Class goes down every Thursday at 10 p.m. and features free whiskey shots served from jockstraps and boozed-up protein shakes. It's a sports bar in the gayest way, where they have "cold pitchers and hot catchers." To go with the theme, they also do 25-cent wing Mondays, will throw a random game on the TVs, and they do bingo on Wednesdays for the kind of jocks who prefer to never break a sweat.

Leave some wiggle room for the good stuff ($9–$11 each) on their regular menu. They always have a couple cocktails that feature aged liquors (like the Fur Trapper) and some that are just straight-up crazy (like the corn-infused, whiskey-based Elote Old Fashioned that'll remind you of the eponymous Mexican street snack, over ice). There's a dollar pool table and photo booth and a giant bench that wraps around the whole place should cocktail hour morph into naptime.

what the fuck is a beer bust?

Both a fund-raiser and a way to get you wasted quickly, a beer bust is a flash event held at local bars where, for an hour or two, you can get $10–$15 bottomless beers on weekends (usually Sundays). Every event's proceeds benefits a different cause, so you can drink your weight in Bud for puppies, down a carafe of Coronas for human rights, and leave feeling like you've done more than liver damage. Check the Facebook pages of 440, Hi Tops, Toad Hall, and Beaux for the next one.

LUCKY 13
#FreeBBQ #Duboce
2140 Market Street

If you're down to your last buck, Lucky 13 will lift your spirits. This bar is best for afternoon drinking and munching on free popcorn, and their happy hour will pull you out of the dumps with $3 beers and $1 goldfish-filled pints. If it happens to be a Saturday, you're in extra luck because they throw a free hot dog and burger BBQ in the yard. It's a biker kind of crowd, which is a lot of fun.

MOBY DICK
#FrozenMargaritas #DickCorral
4049 18th Street

These guys have been dicking around for over thirty years and they have pool, pinball, quiz games, two-for-one frozen drinks (sometimes margaritas, other times Sex on the Beach). There's a huge aquarium in the middle (with dick corral in the middle of that), and sometimes you walk in on crazy shit like a guy wearing only underwear on a platform bed in the back doing some sort of sexy photo shoot on a Monday night.

THE LOOKOUT
#DuboceTriangle #PeopleWatching
3600 16th Street

A second-floor bar with an expansive balcony overlooking the intersection of Market and Castro Streets, the LookOut is right above a fitness store so all the legs you see hanging up there are super buff. You go here for one thing only: drunken people watching. If you can tear yourself away from staring at everyone down below, you'll notice that this bar also comes with panoramic city views. You will never find a seat on the weekend, but come here during weekday happy hour for $4 wells and some primo stalking from above.

THE RESIDENCE
#Duboce #cocktails #chicken
718 14th Street

A sleek and fancy lounge with stylish wallpaper, chic couches and chairs, and Uncle Brother's, the Residence is a fried-chicken pop-up shop that features a different kind of internationally inspired flavor of fried chicken each week (Hawaiian, Southern, Thai, sometimes with waffles). When there's no bird, the house cocktails (average $10) and craft beers are the word. It's a little shabby, a little chic, with a lingering smell of fried chicken.

TWIN PEAKS TAVERN
#HistoricWindow #IrishCoffee
401 Castro Street

Twin Peaks hails from an era when gay bars weren't allowed to show same-sex people intermingling, which means many bars were hidden from sight or went underground. As you'll notice upon entry, Twin Peaks has huge windows up front, which have been saying "Fuck you" to that old law since forever ago (giving it the nickname "the glass coffin"). The interior of this iconic bar hasn't changed much throughout the years and you'll find all that old-fashioned flair on its walls. Hit this place once for the history and twice for the Irish coffee.

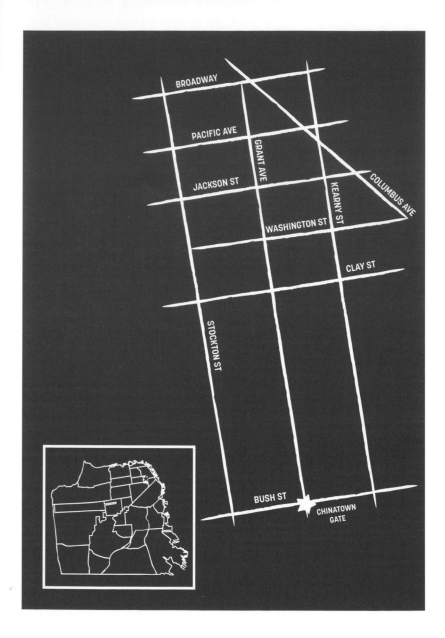

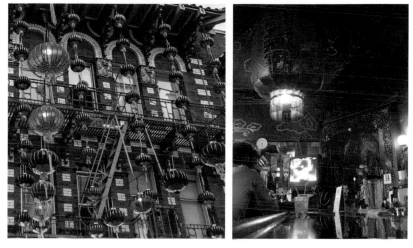

CHINATOWN

The hype makes San Francisco's Chinatown seem huge, but it's relatively small. What it lacks in size, it makes up for in history, density, and charm. All the Chinese businesses here are aware that they're on display for tourists, so you'll rarely find someone who speaks zero English. Despite that fact, the bakeries, restaurants, tea shops, and attractions still hold on to some authenticity. Here, you'll find the best damn egg tarts in the States, dim sum for days, fortune cookies, and old Chinese women running the show. Chinatown used to be completely littered with pink plastic bags that rolled around like the leaves of autumn. Even though California banned plastic bags in 2014, when the wind is just right you'll see a little pink bag float by as a reminder of simpler (less environmentally friendly) times.

COFFEE AND BAKERIES

COOL TEA BAR
#boba #GrassJelly #WiFi
728 Pacific Avenue

In the middle of the madness, you'll find this neon-glowing boba tea shack with courtyard seating (and a few chairs inside). They customize every cup of tea or you can order by number from the top sellers on the menu. These kinds of places are normally too saccharin sweet for our tastes, but at Cool Tea Bar you can customize the sweetness by specifying a percentage (70 percent less sweet is the way to go). Aside from regular tapioca pearls, they also have wiggly grass jelly, which you could get with roasted milk tea.

DESTINY COFFEE AND TEA
#FirmBoba #ChineseHarp
605 Kearny Street

Among the many boba tea shops in the area, Destiny stands out on a few levels. Their boba is on the firmer side and the tea flavors really permeate the milk, especially the jasmine. Their prices are a bit lower ($2–$3) and the shop is much cleaner than other spots. The biggest distinguishing factor is the guy playing a Chinese harp up front. You'll think it's the radio until you see him plucking away rhythmically by the window.

EASTERN BAKERY
#MoonCakes #PorkBuns
720 Grant Avenue

A bakery that has been around almost as long as Chinatown itself, Eastern is the place to go for moon cakes, year-round. If you're not familiar with them, moon cakes are a traditional pastry eaten to promote a good harvest in autumn and are rich, buttery pastries stuffed with a thick lotus paste and egg yolks for prosperity. While tasty, these things will effectively replace your blood with fat if you're not careful. At Eastern, moon cakes come in a variety of flavors and they do you a solid by miniaturizing them. They also sell a bunch of sweet and savory pastries, like coconut bread, fried sesame balls, egg tarts, huge pork buns, and slices of cake for all you super fatties.

GARDEN BAKERY
#PineappleBuns #LoudChineseWomen
765 Jackson Street

The seats at Garden Bakery are consistently packed with Chinese women discussing something loudly over pastries. They make all the traditional pastries, but their pineapple buns are a big standout. While many bakeries focus on the appearance of the top crust, Garden goes for flavor. The crust is flaky and perfect and the 40-cent buns come in three different flavors. Since these buns are so popular here, they bake fresh batches all day to keep up with the demand. Take your fresh-from-the-oven buns to the alley and go to town.

GOLDEN GATE BAKERY
#CultFollowing #EggTarts
#NoDécorAtAll
1029 Grant Avenue

Hands down, Golden Gate is the most popular bakery in Chinatown. You'd think

that with the number of people this place serves, it would be a huge warehouse or at least have some sort of café atmosphere or décor. Nope. It's basically a messy office, littered with pink boxes and run by a few old Chinese ladies. There is no music, no place to sit, and no real display case. You get in line and wait for up to an hour, but will be handsomely rewarded with the best damn egg tart in the world, fresh out of the oven with a flaky crust and perfectly set custard. One woman takes orders and busily boxes while the other works the register with a nonchalant smile. The ladies here are graciously aware that they're famous and they've got an adorable operation going here.

OTP Tip: If you have room, try one of the sesame rice balls. They're slightly greasy, glutinous, generously filled with red bean paste, and collapse lightly with the first bite.

FUN FACT

Pineapple buns never contain any pineapple. It's the cross-hatched design on the crust that gives them their name.

WA LI BAKERY & CAFE
#zongzi #SidewalkPastryHaggling
1249 Stockton Street

Come here for zongzi, a triangular, tamale-like snack wrapped in a lotus leaf. Wa Li has a setup outside with leaves all stacked together in a big pot so you can grab and go if it's too busy inside. You can also get bags of cookies, mini-buns (five for under $2!), and various sweet breads from the lady who monitors the sidewalk.

🍔 EAT

DELICIOUS DIM SUM
#DimSumToGo
752 Jackson Street

This place is tiny, there's a surly lady behind the counter, and seating is practically non-existent. But this isn't some sit-down dim sum palace. This is the kind of place you come to fill a huge bag with shrimp dumplings, shumai, pot stickers, and whatever's left over for under $5, then take the loot to the streets and try not to drop anything.

GOOD MONG KOK BAKERY
#DimSum #PorkBuns
1039 Stockton Street

When you're done being silly about the name, pull out $2 and let's get you fed. The Good ol' Kok is *the* place for pork buns. One of your dollars will go toward a steamed bun with an airy, fluffy shell, stuffed with juicy, flavorful pork. Your other dollar will go toward the exact same bun but baked. These buns are huge and they never skimp on filling. The shrimp dumplings are pretty good, too, but you're here for buns. Focus.

HOUSE OF NANKING
#popular #TryEverything
919 Kearny Street

House of Nanking is a bright red, casual spot where you'll need to loosen the belt two notches before sitting down. This place is popular among the suits and tourists, but legitimately good enough to brave the masses. The tender, steamed-pork dumplings ($8.95) here are a must, as is anything with five spice (pork or fish), and the sesame chicken ($9.95) is perfectly fried and sauced, then served alongside toothsome vegetables. Come here with a larger group, put in an order for the whole menu, and make sure nobody is stingy about sharing.

HOUSE OF XIAN DUMPLING
#SoupDumplings #HandPulledNoodles
925 Kearny Street

Do them the honor of trying the Xian dumplings after which they named their joint. These are life-changing soup dumplings, filled with hot, savory, lip-burning soup that oozes out of the thin dumpling dough. But they don't stop at dumplings. There is a man in a plastic box in the dining room hand-pulling noodles to order, and the best way

to taste his artistry is the beef noodle soup. The place is small, it gets packed for lunch, and slurping is highly encouraged.

HUNAN HOME'S RESTAURANT
#HotAndSourSoup #RealSpice
622 Jackson Street

The décor here is absolutely atrocious. There is no reason why carpet should be that green or the walls that pinkish red, especially together. But hot damn do they have fantastic, authentically spicy Hunan dishes. Here you can try the bolder—actually Chinese—brother of that sad excuse for hot and sour soup you've been eating from plastic containers. A good portion of their menu features spicy dishes tossed with their house hot sauce, which you can adjust based on how much of a baby you are about mouth burn.

LUCKY CREATION VEGETARIAN RESTAURANT
#VegPorkBun #FauxFabulous
854 Washington Street

For all you veg heads who want to play the Chinatown pork bun game, Lucky Creation makes a passable vegetarian version. Get there at 11 a.m. sharp and prepare to be amazed by how flavorful a bun sans meat can be. We've seen places stick bland vegetables in the middle of steamed buns to cater to vegetarians, but this one is a perfectly seasoned, satisfying faux version. Take it to go and eat it alongside your carnivorous friends.

MURACCI'S JAPANESE CURRY & GRILL
#Japanese #curry #katsu
307 Kearny Street

There are times where you find yourself in Chinatown and want nothing to do with Chinese food. For those times, we give you Muracci's, a Japanese curry and katsu lunch joint. This is a fast-food-type place where they make it easy for you to get in and out by offering one beef or chicken curry dish that's ready when you are. If you've got a minute, try the Katsu Don, a breaded and fried pork cutlet over rice with sauce and an egg on top. They spice the curry to your preference and you should get it at full blast.

NEW GOLDEN DAISY
#ChickenWings #ChowMein
1041 Stockton Street

Food here is by the pound and the windows are "decorated" with hanging Peking ducks and other meaty bits. Golden Daisy is all about fried chicken drummettes, which weigh in at $4 per pound. If you think you can polish off an entire pound (about twelve), point and ask the Chinese man to throw them in a white box for you. The skin is always perfectly crispy and, even though it's made in bulk, the chicken is moist and flavorful. Get some BBQ pork chow mein ($2 for a carton) to round out the awful-for-you meal.

NEW LUN TING CAFE
#GreatService #BigPortions #Jello
670 Jackson Street

This is a tiny café with really attentive wait-staff and huge portions. Go to New Lun for the saucy oxtail stew over rice. Then sit back and let the nice lady bring it to you (with free soup sometimes), and pat yourself on the back for only spending $8 on a super-filling lunch. They even throw in a free block of Jell-O at the end of your meal, just for being you.

◉ SEE AND DO

smaller-than-you'd-expect Chinatown Gate stands. Built in the '70s, it is the only North American gate that conforms to Chinese regulations. It looks really strange jammed into the middle of the street and is a cool transition into the bustle of Chinatown.

CHINATOWN ALLEYWAY TOURS
#RunByLocals #CoolHistoryLesson
1525 Grant Avenue

These are not your big, obnoxious bus rides around busy streets. The Alleyway Tours are youth-run and-led, donation-based, and their mission is to share a deeper story of Chinatown, revealed by walking through its back. Tour guides are residents and the program aims to keep the conversation about Chinatown going by training younger kids to be guides and engage in tours. This tour will help you see Chinatown as a distinctive, thriving community and not just as a tourist attraction.

CHINATOWN GATE
#touristy #landmark
Grant and Bush Streets

Take the trolley or hike up the hill to the intersection of Grant and Bush Streets, where the

GOLDEN GATE FORTUNE COOKIE CO.
#FortuneCookies #historic
56 Ross Alley

The fortune cookie does not hail from some Confucian advice giving era of ancient Chinese history. The rumor is that it was invented in San Francisco by a Japanese pastry chef. This little factory, which opens up into the oldest alley in Chinatown, has been a major distributor of the cookies since 1962. Here, you'll walk into a bunch of Chinese ladies screaming at each other in the one-room shop, watch people fold fortunes into hot cookies from their little trays, and pay them the 50 cents they ask per picture. They sell bags of their famous cookies (forty for $3), but also have flat, fortuneless ones, bags of rejects that didn't quite bloom into fortune cookie butterflies, and swirly smakles (like fortune cookie chips).

SHOP

CHINATOWN KITE SHOP
#SoManyKites #FunBrowsing
717 Grant Avenue

If there was ever a time to get really knee-deep into kites, your visit to SF should be it. The weather's just right and this kite store has absolutely every kind of kite you can imagine. Just browsing this place feels like you're on hallucinogens, but if you're serious about getting something to fly high, they'll hook you up. You'll find everything from simple diamond-shaped colorful kites to two-person dancing dragon costumes (not really kites, but somehow in the same category). For $10–$12, you can get yourself something to drag around the sky all afternoon.

PARTYING

BUDDAH LOUNGE

#DiveLounge #dice #Mark

901 Grant Avenue

It is a known fact that the greatest of dives revolves around a divey bartender, and Buddah's got Mark, a man you'll learn to love. The crowd here stumbles in from every which direction and the tourists don't linger long. Do yourself a favor and learn the game of Liar's Dice before coming, then challenge your friends to a few rounds. If you're good, you'll drink yourself bad. If you suck, the drinks you'll have to buy are cheap enough to keep you out of the red.

COMSTOCK SALOON

#NotChinese #cocktails

155 Columbus Avenue

Follow the painted finger pointing you to the front door of this corner cocktail bar. It's not at all Chinese-y and you'll be greeted by a bartender with a bow tie and suspenders, some turn-of-the-century décor, and the kind of vibe that'll make you order something with rye (Sazerac, $9) while stroking your beard. This place is run by some big shots in the bar game (the Absinthe group) and their food is fancy and good.

MR. BING'S

#OldSchoolDive #Bourdain

201 Columbus Avenue

So Anthony Bourdain came here once to "uncover" this dive and now tourists have sniffed out his trail. It sits on the border of Chinatown and North Beach and attracts more drunks from the latter. Despite all this,

Mr. Bing's is a fun spectacle with quirky dive touches (like their ass scratching tennis player lady painting) and cheap drinks. This is the better of the two bars that Bourdain lit up (the other being Li Po, where he got a Mai Tai and now everyone else does, too).

RED'S PLACE

#ChineseDrunks #LoudAndGreat

672 Jackson Street

Old Chinese men actually go here for their cheap drinks, sit around screaming in Mandarin, and then use the wall as a walker until they find the door. Sometimes there's Chinese pop playing on the jukebox, sometimes the screaming gets so loud that it effectively cancels all other noise. Red's has a firm group of regulars, but walking in here doesn't feel all-eyes-on-you awkward. They do cheap beer and shot specials and the bathrooms are the perfect setting for a low-budget horror movie. It's a solid dive through and through.

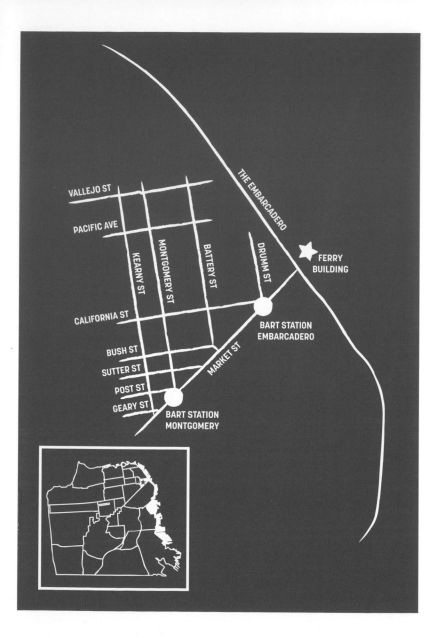

FIDI/

EMBARCADERO

Exploring the Embarcadero is a glorious way to spend the day. The waterfront is always filled with vendors and characters, iconic sculptures (like "Cupid's Arrow"), and a view of the Bay Bridge. The Ferry Building is an incredible collection of the best available artisan goods, fresh-from-the-bay oysters, and picture-perfect produce. As for the financial district right next door, people come here to work. Why are you here? Your motives are to sabotage their lunch break food truck lines and watch them drown their sorrows during happy hour.

COFFEE AND BAKERIES

COFFEE CULTURES
#CounterCultureCoffee
#CleanAndCorporate
225 Bush Street

This small shop is one of the few in SF to serve delicious Counter Culture coffee. The menu looks like a scoreboard and the shop is clean, with corporate-fitting design. Seating is just outdoor chairs and benches. It sits at the bottom of an office building so you'll feel the buzz of the afternoon coffee break crowd.

JACKSON PLACE CAFE
#hidden #BlueBottleCoffee #panini
633 Battery Street

This is a cute place hidden in a courtyard alley with a real Italian man working the espresso machine. We were always under the impression that people from the boot hated hipster coffee, but surprisingly this place serves Blue Bottle coffee. They press a panini like they mean business, and the all-brick interior, accented by real gas lamps, will make you feel worlds away from the FiDi bustle.

MINAMOTO KITCHOAN
#FussyCandy #mochi
648 Market Street

Minamoto is like a Japanese dessert gallery lab, and the ladies working here are all dressed in uniform, which is super intimidating but also cool. They can shape a rice ball into anything and are obsessed with bunny-shaped candy. Their display cases look like they're showcasing jewelry, with jellies glistening in the midafternoon sun. The mochi here is delicate and filled with unique flavors

(like persimmon), and every confection is carefully constructed, likely with tweezers. Taking ridiculous things super seriously is always fun.

THE CHAI CART
#MasalaChai #TinyCartOffTheBart
Embarcadero BART Station

As you step off the BART, you'll be lured by the sweet smell of chai emanating from a tiny cart parked nearby. Follow your nose and you will discover the magic of masala chai, a blend of spices with a ginger-heavy finish, which takes regular chai to a new level. For something milder, the rose chai is floral but still packs a punch. This is a small, one-man operation and the best medicine for the foggy morning blues.

THE STATION SF
#BlueBottleCoffee #ComposedSalads #SidewaysSeating
596 Pacific Avenue

Bulbous subway station lamps light up this corner space, the menu is in block print, and the décor is clean with just one large photo. The Station never fails to smell like bacon, even though they host a pop-up juice company in store. The Blue Bottle iced coffee has the strength of a thousand bulldozers. The salads are amazing and served with fresh bread in winged, sweeping bowls. Pastries, packaged salads, and sandwiches are set up for working people on the run. If it's sunny out, grab a seat on the benches that desperately hug super-slopey Kearny Street to get a real sideways SF experience.

 # EAT

BOCADILLOS
#SanSebastianTapas #wine
710 Montgomery Street

Its name may lead you to believe that Bocadillos is some quick sandwich joint, but it's far from. A romantic Spanish restaurant tucked into a little corner of FiDi, Bocadillos serves substantial tapas inspired by the distinctly different cuisine of San Sebastian. Their giant prawns, grilled à la plancha and topped with tangy lemon confit and garlic, summon thoughts of the northern Spanish coast and the Monterey squid adds a touch of local SF flavor. Order as many plates as you can afford, take long sips of wine in between, and try to stay out of the Scientology church across the street.

BOXED FOOD COMPANY
#GourmetLunchBox #AlleySeating
245 Kearny Street

It doesn't matter if you're staying or going, your lunch will come in a box. Everything here is $10 and their salads and sandwiches are masterpieces of flavor. Boxed Food serves fresh, crispy greens, they roast their vegetables to perfection, they have the juiciest braised tempeh, and they use only high-quality cheeses. Their dressings are balanced and tangy, and adding a little love (avocado) is never a bad idea. While it may look like there's nowhere to sit, if you swing out back there's a beautiful seating area in the alley.

COTOGNA
#TreatYourself #Italian
490 Pacific Avenue

Sitting right next door to two-Michelin-starred restaurant Quince, Cotogna holds its ground in the FiDi fine-dining scene. Michael Tusk runs both restaurants, but the dishes at Cotogna are cheaper, more Italian, and just as good. While the portions are small, the pasta dishes here are divine and coated or stuffed with flavorful, seasonal ingredients. Cotogna offers a prix fixe menu where $28 buys you three courses, allowing you to taste Tusk's talent without all the fuss next door.

GOLD CLUB
#FiveDollarBuffet #FriedChickenFridays
#strippers
650 Howard Street

You don't have to be a Dapper Don to hit up a strip club midday. Gold Club is a classy place with lovely ladies and an all-you-can-eat $5 buffet Monday through Friday from 11:30 a.m. to 2 p.m. You'd think a place that's focused on pole dancing wouldn't take lunch very seriously, but this place is the tits. Their crispy fried chicken is some of the best in the city and they rotate a good selection of sides. Greasy lap dances are optional.

INTERNATIONAL FOOD COURT
#CheapLunch #bibimbap
320 Bush Street

Under a dingy awning and down a flight of stairs, you'll find a sketchy-looking underground cafeteria with some cheap, authentic lunch options. Grandma's spare chairs make up the décor of what feels like a Chinese hospital waiting room with multiethnic vendors lining the perimeter. The Korean stand serves bibimbap for under $10 and the Filipino stand (Lumpia House) is worth the wait.

LIBA FALAFEL TRUCK
#falafel #DIYToppings
#PickledFriedOnions
Location varies

The truck window opens at 11 a.m. and you'll want to hop in the quickly forming line shortly thereafter. Get a salad (which comes with a base of mixed greens, falafel, tahini, and chimichurri for $9), then move to the sidecart to fill 'er up with the sides and toppings. The idea is to pile on inspired sides like Moroccan carrots; beets with orange vinaigrette; chunky eggplant stew; Brussels sprouts with Dijon; cabbage with black sesame; fresh, tangy feta; and roasted peanuts tossed with rosemary, then douse them in squeeze-bottled sauces. Don't forget to throw a giant mound of their brilliant pickled, then deep-fried, red onions on top. At the end of it all, you'll be holding a pound of ridiculously gourmet food and will want to hit the truck for round 2, only to find that their lunch shift is over and the unicorn has galloped to greener pastures.

R&G LOUNGE
#Cantonese #LiveCrab
631 Kearny Street

Around since 1985, this place has grown into a three-level complex of creative cooking. R&G is full of fat-man tourists from the middle of the country who come here for the crab. Battered, spiced with salt and pepper, then deep-fried live, this thing comes to your table and looks you straight in the eye as if it's challenging you. Their other seafood dishes are fantastic as well and the XO sauce is spot-on spicy. The prices are high for Chinese, but you're paying for quality seafood and kill-a-horse portions.

◉ SEE AND DO

EMBARCADERO WATERFRONT

#ScienceMuseum #sculptures
#BayViews

To explore this stretch of promenade along the water, start at Fisherman's Wharf and keep heading down toward the Bay Bridge. Along your walk, you'll find fun attractions like the Exploratorium ($29 entrance fee) at Pier 15, a museum dedicated to the wonders of science and technology, where you'll find projects that'll put your second-grade volcano to shame. When you get too hungry for science, the Ferry Building is right down the promenade and is filled with some of the craftiest food in SF. Further down the route you'll find SOMA, a metal alien spider sculpture that lurks at Pier 14. End your trip at Rincon Park, where the Cupid's Span sculpture will seal the deal on your love affair with SF.

FERRY PLAZA FARMERS MARKET

#Saturday #ProduceBlowOut
#OystersOnThePier
1 Ferry Building

At the Ferry Building, Tuesdays, Thursdays, and Saturday mornings (8 a.m. to 2 p.m.) explode into full market bloom. On the way to the Ferry Building, you'll find hippie jewelry and art vendors lining the sidewalk and King Drum, a man who plays a 360-degree drum set he built from junk, sound-tracking the experience at the intersection. Once you get to the market, prepare to be blown away. In addition to the permanent shops in the building, the outdoor areas are jam-packed with the freshest produce you'll find in California. You can survive off the many free samples or go for clam chowder, rotisserie chicken, fresh oysters, and many other prepared foods. This is one of the more expensive markets in the city, but the quality of their goods is unparalleled.

TRANSAMERICA BUILDING
#IconicStructure #LooksLikeEgypt
600 Montgomery Street

The Transamerica Building was built in 1972 and is an iconic piece of the SF skyline. A giant towering pyramid, the building is covered in crushed, glistening quartz and is topped with a "crown jewel" that lights up on special occasions. At the base, the building has two wings of office space; the forty-eighth floor consists of just one conference room. Its pyramid shape, mocked by some initially, was chosen in an effort to preserve the transmission of sunlight throughout the city. There is a plaque at ground level that pays tribute to two stray dogs (Bummer and Lazarus) that wandered the city in the early 1800s killing rats.

VALLEJO STREET STEPS
#BayViews #BreakASweat

Many people hit these steps from the top down, starting at Russian Hill, but we like to take them on backward. You'll have to hike a 90-degree bitch hill to reach the Vallejo Street steps from the Embarcadero. But it's worth the burn. Continue your ascent up the stairway and watch the beauty of San Francisco unfurl behind you. The Bay Bridge floats up in the distance, the Transamerica Building is on the right, and a garden park full of flowers and well-manicured shrubs surrounds you. Keep looking back as you hike up the stairs for a view that changes with every step up.

Five Ferry Favorites

The Ferry Building is a collection of the best artisanal food SF has to offer, including the freshest oysters in the Pacific at Hog Island Oyster Co. If you've got the cash and physical fortitude, you can spend the whole day eating and buying food-centric gifts, only taking breathers to admire the bay views from the pier.

The sheer amount of stuff packed into the Ferry Building can be intimidating at first. Fear not, food-lover; everything you put in your mouth here is fantastic. But to make it a little more manageable, here are five of our favorites.

ACME BREAD

Pumping out fresh loaves from the hearth oven on site, Acme Bread is an SF staple, and aside from their bakery in Berkeley this is the only place to get everything they offer at its freshest.

COWGIRL CREAMERY

These people wrangle cream into wonderful curds and sell cheese from other fancy producers from all over the world. You can get it by the pound or have it in prepared foods served at Cowgirl Sidekick next door.

HUMPHRY SLOCOMBE

An all-white storefront with daily offerings scribbled on the tiles, Humphry serves the wildest flavors of super-rich and thick ice cream. Try the Guinness Gingerbread or Secret Breakfast.

FAR WEST FUNGI

This store is dedicated to nothing but mushrooms. You'll find them dried in huge jars, fresh and beautiful in little baskets, painted as botanical prints, and in rare bundles under glass. You can even get a grow-your-own-shrooms kit, which are displayed with big-ass mushrooms sprouting from all directions.

PRATHER MEAT

The most respected meat company in SF, this location sells fresh cuts, cured meats, jerky, sausages, and human-grade pet food.

PARTYING

HI DIVE

#WaterfrontSeating #MeatOnSticks
The Embarcadero and Bryant Street

Fashioned like a little grimy boathouse, Hi Dive gives you access to waterfront drinking on their patio as you grab a beer. The menu has fishy, greasy bits and grilled meat on sticks that perfectly complement the setting. You can stick to $3 beers or opt for classier $14 pints of mimosas. Once the view of the bay begins to blur, take a stroll along the Embarcadero to regain your sea legs.

OLD SHIP SALOON

#OldAsFuck #TrueSaloon
298 Pacific Avenue

There are rumors about this being the oldest bar in SF (that title goes to the Saloon in North Beach), and by the looks of it this thing has been around for long enough to say whatever it wants. Originally made from an old ship that crashed around Alcatraz, the Old Ship holds to the tenets of a true saloon, offering bar food (like deep-fried bacon Oreos!), decent beer, and whiskey to enliven even the weariest of sailors. Bring your own loose women.

Hi Dive

Rickhouse

RICKHOUSE
#PunchBowl #libations
246 Kearny Street

Rickhouse has an impressive collection of booze displayed floor to ceiling behind the bar. With this bounty, they make fantastic crafted cocktails for the refined crowd. For sloppy drunks, Rickhouse throws a bunch of alcohol and fruit into a punch bowl ($42 serves a thirsty eight) so that you and your friends can summon memories from freshman year. It's dark and crowded, but there's an upstairs room where you can get shitty on jungle juice until your legs give out.

THE IRISH BANK BAR & RESTAURANT
#IrishPub #AlleySeating
10 Mark Lane

A little Irish pub in an alleyway, serving the type of food you hear about from our friends across the pond. They've got bangers and mash, shepherd's pie, and curry, and the place is plastered with vintage signs and posters. Drinking a Guinness here will feel just right. While the bar is small inside, they take advantage of the alley and use it as their outdoor extension, especially when St. Patrick's Day rolls around.

TROU NORMAND
#charcuterie #brandy
140 New Montgomery Street

Don't come here starving, as their full dinner menu will blow a hole in your pocket. Do come here with a little room for meat. Trou Normand is a special place that revolves around the French idea of having a little brandy and charcuterie between meals. This is a whole-animal establishment; they butcher their meats in-house and turn them into spectacular snacks that pair beautifully with their small selection of cheeses, Acme bread, and rare brandies. Their patio makes for a romantic imaginary journey to northern France.

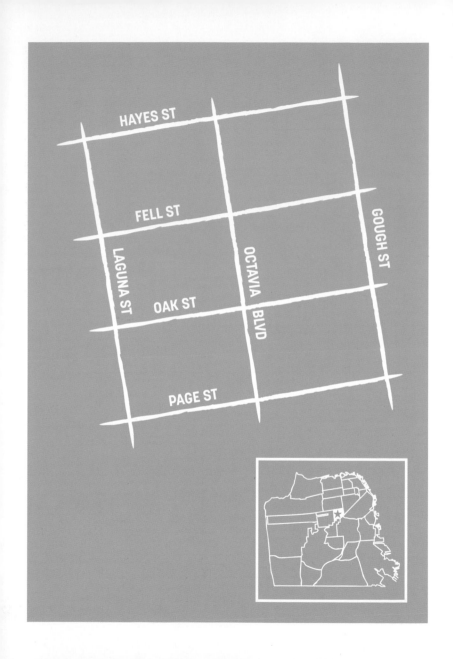

HAYES VALLEY

Hayes Valley is so cute and clever it'll make you nauseous. The neighborhood equivalent of a perfect pantry, you'll find the best craft beer, coffee, ice cream, and desserts here. Just about every café and restaurant in Hayes Valley boasts outdoor seating to promote lounging to the max. The art on the streets is Lego-chic: Here's an entire parking lot full of businesses operating out of shipping containers. Come here for Hayes's popular outdoor beer garden, then hit Ritual Coffee's makeshift container shop and finish off with some nitro-blasted ice cream from Smitten, which is sittin' one box over.

COFFEE AND BAKERIES

ARLEQUIN CAFE & FOOD TO GO
#French #BackyardPark
384 Hayes Street

Arlequin is like a country store with an attached wine cellar. They serve coffee from Sightglass, have inventive pastries, and sell wine by the glass. French posters adorn the walls and the air smells of that good funky old cheese. The big draw here is their backyard, which is more like a park with trees, rocks, vines, benches, and bistro seating all around. The yard is shared with surrounding apartment buildings, giving it a communal vibe.

BLUE BOTTLE COFFEE
#coffee #AlleyWindow
315 Linden Street

Serving that strong delicious brew, this Blue Bottle location is just a walk-up garage window in an alley with concrete blocks set up as alleyway seats. Sipping your coffee here comes with a view. It sits next to a corset shop, where the shopkeeper constantly tightens the corsets, squeezing the doughy mannequin bodies on display in the window. It'll feel good to exhale.

CAFE LA VIE
#BigCups #breezy
514 Octavia Street

The amazing flip-up windows at La Vie let a breeze into the place, and there's sidewalk seating with benches wrapped around trees, perfect for those who enjoy cigs with their coffee. Their coffee is strong; the medium is sixteen ounces(!) and only costs $2. Their pastries sell out early, laptoppers usually fill up the coveted window seats, and the baristas are fast and efficient.

MERCURY CAFE
#DeLaPazCoffee #LocalLunch
201 Octavia Boulevard

A corner spot, you walk into Mercury through a heavy barn door and into a room with awesome local art (robots and nudity, never a bad combo). Radiohead hums through the speakers and the place is open and airy. They brew De La Paz coffee, have freshly prepared scones on the counter, and use the best ingredients they can to make sandwiches, salads, soups, and a fantastic vegan chili. They have pie, local beer on tap, and the crowd ranges from old dudes with newspapers to out-of-work DJs surrounded by their laptop recording studios.

MIETTE
#macarons #chocolates
449 Octavia Street

The fanciest adult candy store ever, Miette offers tiny individually wrapped chocolates, a tin with chocolate sardines, and a gorgeous selection of unique flavors of macarons.

They also sell less fancy candy by the pound, along with flawless cupcakes and actual cake cakes. Everything looks like a French baby made it with its tiny little French baby hands and there's a vintage Schwinn in the window. The guys behind the counter are always happy and high on candy.

RITUAL COFFEE ROASTERS

#ShippingContainer #OutdoorSeating
432B Octavia Street

This location of Ritual is a shipping container that's all decked out in red. Sitting in a parking lot with a basic training course in front of it, you'll get the same great coffee (with select pastries) as you do at their more popular Mission location, but with outdoor quirk. There are lots of chairs and tables around, plus street park seating.

SMITTEN ICE CREAM

#NitroIceCream #ShippingContainer
432 Octavia Street

What if we told you that you can take a tasty liquid, blast it with *Fast and Furious* nitro, and instantly turn it into ice cream?

Smitten makes your molecular dreams come true, plus they bake their own cones, use all-natural ingredients, and are housed in a shipping container. While that may be too many gimmicks for some, missing their salted caramel ice cream ($5 per scoop) on your trip to SF would be like skipping the pyramids in Egypt.

 # EAT

CHEZ MAMAN

#French #TreatYourself
401 Gough Street

The second location of a popular Potrero Hill spot, we dare you to walk by this place and resist going in. The smell of their pungent seafood wafting through the air is intoxicating, and people pick through huge plates of mussels on their sidewalk patio. If you've ever wanted to try escargots (snaily snails), Chez Maman is the place to do it. They also do an amazing Frenched-up burger ($15) for safer eaters.

DRAGONEATS

#cheap #fast #Vietnamese
520 Gough Street

Dragoneats is a well-decorated space with a short menu written on the backdoor chalkboards. An older woman works busily in the kitchen while a younger guy takes orders up front. The food is super fresh, quickly made, and consists of sandwiches, soups, rolls, and bowls. They top most menu items with crispy shallots to take their cheap lunch food ($6–$7) to the next level of awesome.

SOUVLA

#RotatingMeat #Greek
517 Hayes Street

Placing an order here is a bit distracting, as there is an entire wall of rotisserie meat behind the register, rotating in all its juice-dripping glory. Pull yourself together and get some of that meat (leg of lamb, chicken, or pork) thrown over a salad (which is better than the wrap option). The lamb is bathed in a harissa yogurt sauce, then tossed with pickled red onion, feta, and veggies. Load up on hot sauce and try to secure a tiny high barstool up front on the sidewalk.

SUPPENKUCHE

#German #brats #spaetzle
525 Laguna Street

Suppenkuche will ease you into abrasive German cuisine with their pale yellow décor, ceiling of paper butterflies, or—as a last resort—the ample amount of beer on tap. But then you must fend for yourself. It's louder than a thousand canons in there, but you will bear the noise for the chance to sample their moist, lightly breaded pork schnitzel, cheesy spaetzle, and grilled brats (served with tangy kraut and mashed potatoes). Getting a seat here during brunch is like trying to survive a German winter in nothing but a nightgown.

👁 SEE AND DO

CITY RIDE BIKE RENTALS
#ShippingContainer #NotFuglyBikes
370 Linden Street

City Ride Bikes is a shipping container bike shop with a massive inventory of bikes, considering the space limitations. Plus, these aren't dorky clunkers, either; they stock legit bikes that you'd be proud to call your own, even if it's only for a day. Every rental comes with a helmet, a map, a lock, and sage advice. It's only $32 to rent a basic city bike for the day (or $225 for the entire month) and you get 20 percent off if you book online.

SHOP

CARRY LANE

#DiscountDesigner #RunwayStyles
560 Laguna Street

Down a few steps in the basement, you'll find a store with insane prices on designer samples. Given its position among expensive stores on the Hayes strip, you'll think you can't afford anything in here. It may look like it came off the runway (hint: Some of it did), but the prices are rock bottom because they get samples and overstock from designers and sell them for up to 80 percent off. You'll find top-quality fabrics and funky runway styles with an even split of men's and women's clothing and accessories. All items in stock are out on the floor and they get new styles every week. Their Mission and Inner Richmond locations follow the same resale rules and have similar inventory.

OTP Tip: You get 10 percent off when you pay with cash.

TRUE SAKE

#SingleServingSake
560 Hayes Street

An entire store dedicated to Japan's drink of choice, True Sake offers an amazing selection of nothing but sake and serving accessories for this Japanese staple. While there are a lot of expensive bottles around, True Sake also carries single-serving juice boxes and individual sealed glass jars that'll run you $3–$9. Every item has washers around it with note cards, some with information about how to sneak booze into sporting events. The employees here are passionate about sake and will give you the full rundown if you ask.

PARTYING

BIERGARTEN

#ShippingContainer #beer #pretzels
424 Octavia Street

Owned by the same people as the German brunch spot Suppenkuche (page 76), this shipping container beer garden serves warm pretzels, sausages, and great beer in a casual outdoor picnic setting during the day. It's just a little courtyard set up in a concrete parking lot space with lights strewn about, and the vibe is always relaxed. They did an excellent job working within the confines of the space and deserve at least one toast.

BRASS TACKS

#GlassLight #cocktails
488A Hayes Street

Their impressive lighting fixture—made of upside down hanging glasses—will mesmerize you, more so after downing a few of their cocktails, like the Beetle Juice. The bartenders here are true booze artists and will cook you up a drink if you give them a little info about what you like and how you're feeling (our go-to is mezcal and wildebeest-ly).

HOTEL BIRON

#HiddenWineBar #DateDungeon
45 Rose Street

If you've scored yourself a date, Hotel Biron will help you seal the deal. You will walk through a small alley, and just when your date thinks her ankles are about to be slashed, you'll step into a dim, brick-and-wood room, covered in eclectic wall art. Take a seat on the couch, and order a few meats and cheeses and a couple glasses of the

classy stuff. The prices here (starting at $12 a glass) are steep, but the experience, quality, and turbo boost of your coolness is worth it.

RICKSHAW STOP

#DanceParty #LiveMusic
155 Fell Street

Take the one-eyed octopus painted on the outside as an indicator of the crazy times to be had inside. This is a small club with padded walls and zero ventilation. They put on live music and dance parties that get wild and loud fast. A layer of back sweat will form the minute you step in, and their cheap drinks will fuel the dance fire and keep it rolling all night. Be warned that this is an eighteen-plus venue, so check for wristbands before pulling out your best moves.

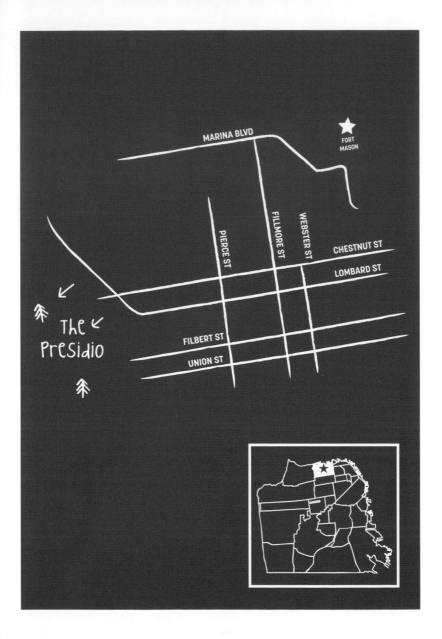

MARINA/
COW HOLLOW

Think of the Marina this way: Ken and Barbie built a Malibu
dream house and populated it with spoiled, crying babies.
You'll find people closing deals via earbuds in their PJs
and tourists walking around trying to figure out why their
currency exchanged to nothing here. The bros come out at
night (or anytime there's a Giants game) with their BMWs
and flashy watches. The locals drink Starbucks and spend
way too much on dinner, but you're smarter. Roll through
the Marina on your way to OTG, the most amazing Friday
evening food truck event with music and good, cheap food
that'll put all those chichi restaurants to shame.

COFFEE AND BAKERIES

BEREKA COFFEE
#SingleCupBrew #Ethiopian
2320 Lombard Street

A tiny to-go sliver of a place with no seating, Bereka closes super early (3 p.m.), so come here for your morning coffee and breakfast sandwich. The kind ladies behind the counter understand that you're jet-lagged and incomprehensible, and they'll brew you a personal drip cup of the strongest Ethiopian coffee to help ease you into the day.

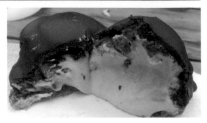

PACIFIC PUFFS
#CreamPuffs #GanacheCovered
2201 Union Street

Cupcake makers, beware: The cream puff is the new kid in town. The pâte à choux is so delicate and the custard-cream filling so light that it'll feel like you're eating a bunny hug. For $3.25 a puff, you can get them with Madagascar vanilla cream, powdered sugar, chocolate cream, and slathered with ganache, or with a fruity strawberry filling. Or opt for a tiny mini-puff (for just $2).

KARA'S CUPCAKES
#FancyCupcakes #AmazingFrosting
3249 Scott Street

If you're still stuck in the 2010 cupcake craze, Kara is right there with you, making the fancy cupcakes and displaying them like Fabergé eggs behind glass. When everyone else has moved on to other pastries, Kara still labors over her cupcakes, creating moist little cakes in flavors like Key Lime Pie, Kara's Karrot (with luscious cream cheese frosting), and Chocolatey S'mores. Cupcakes are Kara's canvas and the lady's got some Picasso-esque skills.

WRECKING BALL COFFEE
#ExpertCoffee #LikeScienceButTasty
2271 Union Street

This minimalist shop looks like a coffee lab and their offerings taste like science. Other than the pineapple print wallpaper, everything else is stark white and you'll get that nervous feeling that you'll be the asshole who spills coffee on the pristine counter. You will not want to spill this coffee. Wrecking Ball is run by people with top coffee credentials (both partners are board members of the World Barista Championship) and they source and roast their owns beans. Get a cappuccino and hold on tight; this is going to be a journey into coffee paradise.

🍔 EAT

BAKER STREET BISTRO
#French #PrixFixe
2953 Baker Street

This place will normally suck your wallet dry, but we found its dirty little secret: a prix fixe menu that'll score you four courses for $20. It's only available Tuesday to Thursday and Sunday, but you'll get a masterfully prepared soup, salad, plate of the day, and dessert. When their Mussels Provençale alone run a cool $20, this is one of the best deals in town. Desserts are all French fancy and their wine selection ($9-$10 per glass) is top-notch.

CASTANGA
#TreatYourself #French #beignets
2015 Chestnut Street

A simple, tall, red exterior banner draws your eye into this pinky-up French spot. It's stylish but not snooty with a huge wine rack inside. Don't go too crazy on getting a lot of food (you can't afford it anyway). Instead, a simple niçoise salad or a hunk of lasagna served with greens will leave you with just enough room for their flight of beignets (caramel apple, Nutella, and vanilla), which will ruin American doughnuts for you forever.

CAUSWELLS
#SmallPlates #DoughnutBreadPudding
2346 Chestnut Street

Causwell's is comfortable and laid-back, with small plates ($9-$15 each) that feature beautifully prepared chanterelles, slightly spicy octopus, and shrimp over grits, among others. The portions aren't tiny, but you'll want to get several dishes and share. Their doughnut bread pudding, however, you should tackle on your own.

THE SANDWICH SPOT
#BigSandwiches #BeachHutFeel
3213 Pierce Street

A welcome departure from sport coat snobs, their motto "Love all, feed all" is written above the door and the whole place has a beach hut vibe. While nobody really surfs in the Marina, wearing your board shorts at the Sandwich Spot won't be frowned upon. The sandwiches here are stuffed with meat, have creative names, and all cost less than $8. The Horny Hapa is like Thanksgiving year-round, the Manwich is loaded with three kinds of meat (pastrami, roast beef, and salami), and the My Cousin Vinny is a nod to the classic Italian meatball sub.

THE TIPSY PIG
#brunch #cocktails #patio
2231 Chestnut Street

A bar with tasty food, The Tipsy Pig has a juicy burger ($14) that'll cure whatever ails you on a Sunday morning. Shoot past the bar and onto their patio, order one of those bad boys with an egg on top ($2 extra) for a brunchier feel and pair it with the Strawberry Fields cocktail, which is made with our favorite vodka (Russian Standard). The crowd is young (and sometimes dumb), but this burger will save the day.

YUKOL PLACE THAI CUISINE
#Thai #MangoStickyRice
2380 Lombard Street

Yukol is pretty standard Thai fare in an area that's sorely lacking in this kind of cuisine at reasonable prices. You've got your spring rolls, curries, spicy beef salads, and noodle dishes, and dinner can be had for $11–$15. The ingredients are fresh, the mango sticky rice is legit, and they'll adjust the spice levels based on your preference.

ZUSHI PUZZLE
#LiveUni #TreatYourself
#MakeReservations
1910 Lombard Street

Elbow your way through the khakis and expensive manicures to get to the live uni, and if you've never had it fresh, this will be something to remember. Served in the shell (at market price, between $15 and $17), the flavor is distinctive, with an unbelievably creamy texture. The chef, Roger Chong, is actually Chinese but well trained in the sushi arts by a Japanese master. If you've got the bucks to back it, get the sashimi platter, where the chef picks ten ($21), twenty ($39), or thirty ($56) pieces of the freshest fish they've got. If you're not a purist, their anniversary roll—albacore accented by ponzu and bonito flakes—is great. The place is small and you'll need to make a reservation.

◎ SEE AND DO

LYON STREET STEPS
#workout #view

Hike all the way up Green Street until you hit Lyon Street. Surrounded by lush gardens, these steps will give you a view of Alcatraz and the rest of the city on a clear day. The entire ascent is broken in half so you can take a much needed breather in the middle. Here, you'll also find one of several heart sculptures, installed in 2004. If you're not already in love with San Francisco, you'll have a hard time fighting the feels up here.

OLD VEDANTA TEMPLE
#HinduTemple #InsaneArchitecture
2961 Webster Street

The craziest-looking thing you'll see in the Marina is this relic of a temple. Said to be the oldest Hindu temple in the Western Hemisphere, the Old Vedanta is a shocking piece of architecture in the middle of a residential part of the neighborhood. Perpetually under construction, it's currently vacant but stands there majestically mocking the rich bitches with its unattainable beauty.

WAVE ORGAN
#WaterSoundPipes #QuirkyArt
1 Yacht Road

Sponsored and built by the Exploratorium in 1986, the wave organ is a unique San Francisco creation. The organ consists of several pipes to capture the sounds of the ocean crashing against the rocks. There's a stone bench down there, and once you get cozy (and a little wet) you can experience the unreal symphony of the ocean. The sound is best during high tide when the ocean has all its fingers in play, but by shoving your ear into the listening pipes you'll suck some sounds from the waves any time of day.

WTF iS OTG?

Off the Grid (OTG) is an organization after our hearts, bringing "roaming mobile food extravaganzas" to various parts of SF on a regular basis. Not just a collection of the best food trucks in town, OTG also brings with it DJs, booze, games, and experiences. They hold picnics in the Presidio, feed the masses downtown, and spice up SOMA. Our favorite is their setup at Fort Mason every Friday night (5 to 10 p.m.). In the Marina, a place where affordable dining options are scarce, this celebration of cheap eats is much needed. While you can't get a bad bite here if you tried, these five trucks are legendary and not to be missed.

THE CHAIRMAN TRUCK

The Chairman's tiny little buns (served steamed or baked) are absolute perfection. There are just five choices and if you only have room for one, go for the pork belly, a fatty piece of pork perfectly accented by crispy, pickled diakon. Fuck it, get the spicy chicken one, too.

KOJA KITCHEN

An interesting fusion of Korean and Japanese food, Koja is like the samurai of food trucks with the fanciest flat-screen menu display. The best thing here is the Koja beef, a burger stuffed with saucy rib chunks and served between two rice cakes.

SEÑOR SISIG

This truck is bringing the joy of sisig, a Filipino happy hour food normally made with pig head parts, to the masses. They swap in pork shoulder but maintain the traditional spices of their father's family recipe. Get it in a burrito or a taco, over nachos, or as a rice plate, and prepare to be blown away by the flavor.

PINOY LECHON BBQ & GRILL

You can smell Lechon's slow-roasting pork throughout the fort, and for $10, they slice it fresh from the rotisserie and onto your plate.

THE CRÈME BRÛLÉE CART

This is the creamy, custardy, slightly burnt dessert of your dreams and now you don't have to go anywhere near a fine-dining restaurant to get one.

HONORABLE MENTION

BACON BACON

Bacon Bacon is a big, black intimidating truck with a bacon-loving dude standing out front to take orders. Try the bacon-fried chicken ($9.75), porky fries ($7), and pork belly sliders.

OTP Tip: Stand-up tables with heaters overhead are spread out around the fort, but the best place to sit is up at the top of the food fest pit under the windswept trees, looking out into the bay. Get a cocktail ($10). And bring a sweater.

Hike it Out in the Presidio

The Presidio is San Francisco's outdoor gym, a network of trails that range in difficulty and have incredible views. Come here to break in your sneakers and make the requisite trek across the Golden Gate Bridge.

GETTING THERE

Various buses will get you here, but to do it for free, PresidiGo is a shuttle that departs from downtown (Drumm and California, near the Embarcadero BART station) every thirty minutes on weekends. It's a big, comfy tour bus and will take you right into the middle of the park by the band barracks, where trumpet wake-up calls were how soldiers started their days up until the '70s. The whole area is built on former military grounds, so you'll get a lot of history tidbits with your hikes.

PARK TRAIL

An easy 1.7-mile, mostly flat walk, this trail runs through the center of the Presidio. On the way, you can hit up Crissy Field, a historic former airfield where people now like to eat their lunch. You can also explore the National Cemetery, where female spies, Civil (and other) War vets, and Buffalo Bills (African-American soldiers, as named by the Native Americans) are buried. Frederick Funston—the big earthquake hero who also has a street named after him—is here, too.

BATTERY TO BLUFFS TRAIL

This is a short trail (0.7 miles) with a bunch of stairs that hug the rocky Pacific coast. Baker Beach, the birthplace of Burning Man, is accessible from the sand stairs located at the north end. Be warned, though: This part of the beach is notorious for naked old people.

OPEN UP THAT GOLDEN GATE

The Bay Area Ridge Trail is your golden ticket to the bridge. Along this gorgeous, 2.5-mile trail you'll see lush forests, cliff ridges, and the larger-than-life sculptures of Andy Goldsworthy integrated into the scenic landscape. This trail extends across the Golden Gate Bridge and the view of it on approach will make your heart skip. Before hopping on the bridge, check out Fort Point, an overlook with interactive scale models of the bridge (one is all steel and movable) and 3D renditions of the ocean floor made of stone. This is where you take your cliché tourist picture with the bridge serving as background to your windblown face. Once you're on the Golden Gate, the views will include Alcatraz, sailboats, seals bitch-slapping seagulls, and occasional surfers. It's windy as fuck up there and will take you about forty minutes to get across on foot.

OTP Tip: Rent a bike at Sports Basement for $15 for three hours or a GoPro for $35 a day. There are bike paths all around the trails, and if you're biking across the bridge, Marin County will be easier to explore by bike on the other side.

PARTYING

CAMPUS
#FreeSnacks #AnimalAss
2241 Chestnut Street

Game days at Campus are packed and awful. Instead, come here on weekday afternoons when you can take advantage of the step-up-from-Lunchables meat and cheese tray they put out for everyone to munch on. They've got Fernet on tap, along with reasonably priced drinks ($7–$9). There are taxidermied animal asses on the walls and the ladies behind the counter are always pleasant, even when the bros invade.

MAUNA LOA
#SortOfSurfThemed #BuckHunter
3009 Fillmore Street

Around since 1939, Mauna Loa is loosely surf-themed with a huge turtle shell and a few surfboards scattered on the walls. Their happy hour runs until 8 p.m. on weekdays with $4 wells and $1-off drafts. After happy hour, a total shift in both staff and crowd happens. All of the dads (and the older bartender) disappear into the fog and a bearded kid takes over the throttle, with a lady friend for backup. Nirvana, Garbage, and Alice in Chains find their way out of the jukebox; the pool table and shootout basketball game start getting some action; and Buck Hunter gets manhandled.

THE BLACK HORSE LONDON PUB
#MicroscopicBar #BeerTub
1514 Union Street

We've been to bathrooms bigger than this bar, and given that The Black Horse serves its beers from a bathtub, we're not entirely sure this joint isn't actually a bathroom. Since you'll have to negotiate elbow room, there's no way you'll leave this place without making friends (or mortal enemies). There are only eight beers (and nothing else) and they only accept cash.

Campus

THE INTERVAL AT LONG NOW
#SecretBar #SpaceNerds #coffee
2 Marina Boulevard, Building A

If you're a giant space geek, The Interval is hidden in Building A in the back of Fort Mason and will blow your little nerd brain. Set up like some spacey architect's loft living room, the bar is good for a glass of wine (or coffee) and deep conversation around the orrery, a device that predicts planetary positions. There's also an all-glass communal table so you can take a seat when your scrawny little legs give out.

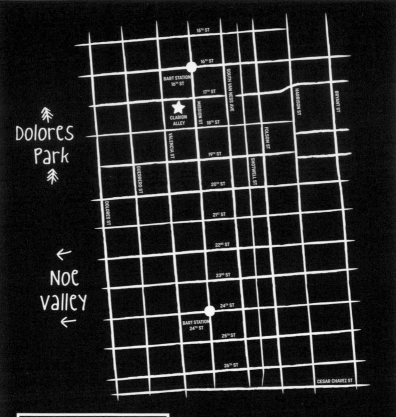

15TH ST

16TH ST

BART STATION
16TH ST

17TH ST

★
CLARION
ALLEY

18TH ST

19TH ST

20TH ST

21ST ST

22ND ST

23RD ST

24TH ST

BART STATION
24TH ST

25TH ST

26TH ST

SOUTH VAN NESS AVE

HARRISON ST

BRYANT ST

FOLSOM ST

SHOTWELL ST

MISSION ST

VALENCIA ST

GUERRERO ST

DOLORES ST

CESAR CHAVEZ ST

Dolores
Park

← Noe
Valley
←

MISSION

There's a duality to the Mission. On the one hand, the Mission is a historically Mexican neighborhood, boasting bright Chicano murals on storefronts, roaming Mariachi bands playing inside restaurants, and the best burritos in the world. On the other, young people with money are moving into newly built condos and pouring their Google paychecks into fancy restaurants. While tension about gentrification is high, the lines blur at the borders and a sense of community perseveres. This place has so much soul. From a man who rides his Segway decked out in sports memorabilia, bumpin' 2PAC, and with a small dog under his arm, to the megaphone-wielding Jesus freak at the 16th Street BART station, the Mission is undoubtedly filled with characters.

COFFEE AND BAKERIES

BI-RITE CREAMERY
#IceCream #famous
3692 18th Street

This is the most popular ice cream place in San Francisco and their lines get so long that they pull out the red ropes to keep the sidewalk manageable. It's a tiny shop that's a spin-off of the market across the street. While the market has been around since the '40s, the (all-organic and local) Creamery first opened its doors to ice cream fiends in 2006. Instead of mucking it up with lots of things, Bi-Rite only uses five ingredients or less and focuses on extracting intense flavors from them. Their salted caramel tastes like the center of a Cadbury Creme Egg, but in rich, cold, ice cream form.

CRAFTSMAN & WOLVES
#CrazyCombos #ElevatedBakedGoods
746 Valencia Street

The pastries here seem like the product of taking shrooms in the walk-in fridge of a Parisian restaurant. Craftsman & Wolves offers twisted spins on French-American-fused baked goods. Some of their pastries look familiar, others are all wacked-out and reimagined into something spectacular. An average muffin may have a runny egg inside, their tarts will hide a bit of eucalyptus, and the cakes are square. What this place does with croissants is absurd. Craftsman & Wolves brings a new level of creativity to a city that's deadly serious about its baked goods.

CREAM
#IceCreamSandwiches #DIY
3106 16th Street

CREAM (Cookies Rule Everything Around Me) gets the money, dollar dollar bills (like $4-$6 per sandwich), ya'll! There's nothing better than an ice cream cookie sandwich late at night. You pick your cookie, then stuff it with your choice of ice cream, then roll it in a topping. There are a lot of sugar-high teenagers here at all times and the ice cream is on the sweet side, but when that craving hits, CREAM is a better option than the corner-store freezer.

DYNAMO DONUT AND COFFEE
#famous #WildFlavors #FluffyAsFuck
2760 24th Street

Owner Sara Spearin started this doughnut

shop when she was pregnant, which explains the crazy-ass flavors. While her (not as simple as it sounds) Vanilla Bean is the classic and most popular, there's a board of daily flavors featuring things like Grapefruit Campari, Chocolate Rose, and I'm Not a Gluten Chocolate with Raspberry Black Pepper Glaze. Every doughnut is unique, handmade, and fluffy as fuck. The shop serves Four Barrel coffee and has a little patio along with a walk-up window on 24th Street where you can get your doughnuts and run.

FAYE'S VIDEO & ESPRESSO BAR
#videos #coffee #gifts
3614 18th Street

A tiny espresso bar jammed into an obsolete video rental place, Faye's is a charming oddity. While you can actually rent videos of all kinds with specials every day (like $2 Mondays or documentary Tuesdays), the films serve more as nostalgic décor. The

coffee is McLaughlin and the espresso bar has a modern yet old-timey feel. Living up to its motto of "All kinds of films, all kinds of formats, all kinds of friendly," Faye's has a charismatic barista, who pulls your shots to perfection every time. They also sell quirky merch like a water glass labeled "Not Google Glass," pencils, magnets, and pencil-drawn character art.

FOUR BARREL COFFEE
#FamousCoffee #RoastingPlant
375 Valencia Street

Four Barrel is right at the center of the love/hate relationship the Mission has with imminent gentrification. Regardless of the politics, this place is nothing short of spectacular. The outdoor seating hits you first, with an industrial chic arrangement of steel and wood and a bike rack built right in. Upon entering, you'll feel transported to a twisted barn with angry taxidermied pig heads on the wall, wound-up rope lights, a wooden vaulted ceiling, a record library, and butcher-block tables. There's a pour-over station where people stand around talking shop, and the main counter is a busy swarm of baristas, pulling shots with serious precision. All their roasting happens in the back in huge industrial barrels, and you can watch the action from strategically placed tables. Four Barrel is perpetually busy, even without WiFi.

HAUS COFFEE
#LaptopCity #RitualCoffee
#DeLaPazCoffee
3086 24th Street

A lofty coffee shop with better-than-Ikea décor that's less a haus and more a laptop farm. The interior is bright and open, with light wood, recessed lighting, and an expansive yard. The coffee is strong, they know

mint combined with coffee (sorry, no booze) and tastes like an Andes mint. While older coffeehouses struggle to keep up with the times, Philz's unconventional coffee and haphazard décor keep the coffee freaks happy.

RITUAL
#SnobCoffee #NoWiFi
1026 Valencia Street

Do you love coffee? We mean really love it? Like if you had a baby with coffee, you would get your tubes tied in fear that your womb would be polluted by something that could never live up to coffee? Well, Ritual loves their coffee in this way. For the average Joe, this place feels like snob city, but once you wrap your mouth around their espresso, pourovers, or immaculate pastries, you'll understand the hype. They coddle their beans and serve the extractions with a bit of know-it-all pretension. Unplug and enjoy a perfect cup of coffee because they don't do WiFi.

STABLE CAFE
#FairytaleYard #coffee #WineWithLunch
2128 Folsom Street

This place is primo for Euro lunch and offers a romantic deal: two sandwiches or paninis and a bottle of wine for $25. They serve De La Paz coffee, pastries, bread pudding, and ten different cookie varieties. The big draw of this

how to make a proper cappuccino, and they feature various roasts from De La Paz and Ritual. There are plenty of outlets that help water the laptop farm and the tunes are so mellow they're barely considered sounds.

PHILZ
#MintMojitoIcedCoffee #FirstLocation
748 Van Ness Avenue

You think you know Philz, but you have no idea. It looks like a chain because it's aesthetically similar to Peet's, but once you walk in it's nothing you'd expect. It starts with a story of a man named Phil who laid down his bean roots on 24th Street when all the hipster cafés were still breast-feeding. Phil does things differently; there is no espresso here and you line up in front of a horde of busy baristas (as you would in a deli) until one is available to serve you. They brew one cup at a time to your specifications. The popular mint mojito iced coffee consists of muddled whole place is their huge open yard, which is also a garden gallery showcasing the skills of Lila B, a landscape artist. Cactus creations and plant displays set the scene with a pebble-filled floor, trees everywhere, little strung-together lights, swooping overhead canvas triangles to keep out the elements, and stable doors that open out into the sidewalk. It feels like a country-home-living catalog and smells like smoked meat and gouda.

STANZA
#coffee #FancyDécor #backyard
3126 16th Street

Do you need to have huge booths and ornate Moroccan lighting to complement your coffee and laptopping needs? Seating and outlets are plentiful here, and there's a whole wraparound booth area out back for hanging like an international drug kingpin. Aside from the plush surroundings, Stanza has fantastic coffee from Kuma, Huckleberry, and De La Paz that they whip into whatever beverage you'd like. The pastries

(popovers, doughnuts, and muffins) are carefully displayed under the counter glass and the cold-brew drip machine is worked into the condiments station so you can see the magic happen as you stir in your milk. This place is solid and their Haight location (1673 Haight Street) is dolled-up in a whole different—but just as fancy—theme.

SUGARLUMP
#coffee #fireplace #mod
2862 24th Street

Sugarlump has the feel of a mod living room from the '60s with leather swivel chairs; several communal tables and couches; low-hanging sassy, chic lamps; and a bulbous fireplace right in the center. Their pastries are from Bernal Heights' Sandbox Bakery, known for their buttery croissants, scones, and morning rolls. Even at the crack of dawn, the barista is pleasant and quick-witted. They aren't jerks about laptop lingerers and provide plenty of outlets for doing the same.

TARTINE BAKERY
#famous #MorningBuns
#AncientGrainBread
600 Guerrero Street

San Francisco stands in line better than any other place, and if you'd like to test your patience, do it at Tartine for a flaky, perfect morning bun. One of the most famous Bay Area bakeries, Tartine isn't just about sweets. The co-owner, Chad Robertson, spent time in Denmark digging through grains and learning about older varieties before bringing them back into his kitchen to bake up some bad-ass bread. You can have it as a loaf or get them to make you a sandwich; either way, this bread is unique and each loaf's distinctive flavors will change the way you think about grains.

 # EAT

BLOWFISH SUSHI
#SushiClub #anime
2170 Bryant Street

This place has been doing sushi differently for years. They've got the nutty rolls Americans go crazy for and some fresh fish to satisfy the purists. But the draw here is the clublike atmosphere that comes with your meal. Blowfish goes out of their way to be loud and bright, creating a hectic Tokyo-inspired atmosphere backed by sassy DJs and anime on the walls. It gets pricey but comes with a party.

BOOGALOOS
#LazyBreakfast #CoolOldSpace
3296 22nd Street

Crammed into an old pharmacy (with vintage signage intact), this is the kind of breakfast joint where you fall out of bed and plop into a diner booth. They've got the requisite cheap pancakes, waffles, eggs, and bacon. The coffee is crap and they refill it in rounds. You don't really have to wear shoes nor be very coherent at this solid breakfast diner. The only thing missing is a server named Flo.

CHINO!
#BobaWithBooze #Chineseish
3198 16th Street

Chino! serves gringo-Mission Mex/Chinese fusion in an appropriately eclectic setting with technicolor lamps around the bar, paintings of old Chinese men against neon backgrounds on the walls, Hello Kitty décor up front, pink sneakers hanging from the web of light-cicles, rainbow chopsticks, and utensils in table holes. Their funny menu features small portions of pork riblets, halibut ceviche, chicharon-laced bao, and comes with an information page explaining how to eat their XLB dumplings without burning your mouth. Mexicans make most of the food in the open kitchen, with the exception of Leo Gan, the dump "king," who crafts dumplings in his own isolated station. It may be too loud and kitschy for some, but we dig it because we like fun.

DELFINA
#FamousFood #pizza #pasta
#TreatYourself
659 Valencia Street

This restaurant group owns two side-by-side spots: One's a fancy pizzeria, the other is a sit-down Italian joint, and neither is cheap. The pizzeria serves the kind of pies that need to be elevated on a little stand, both to symbolize their being inches above the competition and just to be closer to your nose. The crusts are thin and charred with a balanced sauce and the finest toppings.

The sit-down joint uses some of the freshest ingredients around and finagles them into delicate pasta, fish, and vegetable dishes. The kind of stuff that lightly pinches every one of your taste buds and doesn't let up until you're out the door.

FOREIGN CINEMA
#TreatYourself #BookInAdvance
2534 Mission Street

This is one of the Mission's most talked-about restaurants. Reservations are taken a month in advance (especially for brunch) and we think dinner is the way to see Foreign Cinema at its romantic best. The space is industrial chic with a giant, open warehouse courtyard sprinkled with lights and heaters, which screens indie films. There's also an art gallery open to the public and upper-level seating if you're the nosy, stalking type. The food is Cal-Mediterranean, and while it

changes daily, the chefs here have been kicking ass since 1999 so you can rest assured that your money will be deliciously spent.

OTP Tip: Want to continue blowing money on booze? Nightly after-dinner parties are held at their adjacent bar, Lazlo.

LAZY BEAR
#ReallyTreatYourself
#SecretDinnerPartyGoneLegit
3378 18th Street

Lazy Bear started as a secret dinner party and keeps hints of its roots in this brick-and-mortar operation. The chef never went to culinary school and Lazy Bear is a product of his love for food as art and his desire to share the entire process with his guests. Dinner starts like a house party with expertly crafted punch and amusing snacks served on the upper balcony from where you watch

the open kitchen prepare for service. When dinner commences, you'll be treated to a completely different fine-dining experience. The seating is communal, each chef explains their vision behind every course, guests are encouraged to ask questions and walk into the kitchen, and Lazy Bear (chef/owner David Barzalay) himself makes a heartfelt speech come dessert time. The entire experience lasts about three hours, costs $150 (without cocktails), and is a voyeuristic symphony that's innovative fine dining with a renegade underground edge.

LOLO

#InsaneDécor #MexicanTapas
974 Valencia Street

The food here is inventive Mexican served tapas-style, with an assertive kick of acid that matches the tripped-out décor. There are men's sport coats plastered to the booths with a Warhol repetition of found items like baskets of fake flowers, tiny boots in tires, and dog statues watching over the front door. Hanging blue buckets accented with pom-poms light up the bar, which is set against the backdrop of stock images of palm trees and a sunset blown up to huge proportions. Like Dali's clashy, chic basement arranged by some kid with OCD, LoLo leaves a visual impression, even though the food's hit or miss.

LOS SHUCOS

#LatinDogs #StreetFood
3224 1/2 22nd Street

Our most lucid dreams involve street hot dog vendors all uniting in one place, selling those amazing cart dogs you pick up after a night of getting shitty at the club. Shucos captures the club parking lot at 2 a.m. smell, with bacon and onions in the air, but minus the barf on our breath. Plus, they bring crazy toppings—like pineapple and chorizo—to the party and call their dogs funny names (like Tia Juana). La Llorona is the closest to the street dog we are used to, but the others are just as good.

OTP Tip: If Shucos is shut down for the night, you can always get your late-night bacon-wrapped hot dog fix from the cart along Mission Street near 20th Street.

MAU

#Vietnamese #SitDown
665 Valencia Street

A large, modern Vietnamese place with the standard Americanized favorites, but also with some standouts like frog legs and whole fried fish. If you can forget about the hideous mural in the back, the ambience is quite nice and their food is mighty tasty. Their spring rolls are addicting; the tofu bun is a steaming combo of veggies, crispy tofu, and herbs

over rice; and their brisket bánh mì is a two-fister, packed with meat and flavor. The servers are mostly thirty-year-old white guys (as is the crowd), but the food still maintains some level of authenticity, although at higher prices.

MISSION BANH MI
#KoreanGroceries #BánhMì #burgers
2200 Mission Street

Inside a mostly Korean supermarket, with all kinds of crazy shit like big fanned out taro leaves and buckets of gojuchang, you will find Mexican ladies making $5 Vietnamese sandwiches, summer rolls, and salads (papaya, seaweed, and kale). Plus, you can get burgers and vegan tofu portobello sandwiches. There's a little seating area where you can enjoy your market finds. It makes zero ethnic sense, but it's great nonetheless.

MISSION CHINESE FOOD
#PretendDive #FamousFood
2234 Mission Street

To the untrained eye, this place is a hole in the wall with surprisingly good, spicy Chinese food. In reality, famous chef Danny Bowien loosely disguised this shop under the original restaurant signage (Lung Shan Restaurant) to create a dining sensation. There are no old Chinese women serving you here (just hipster girls), the menu isn't newspaper length, and the music is mostly old school hip-hop. Mission Chinese serves a limited selection of ballsy, can't-stop-eating-it-like-a-bag-of-hot-Cheetos, Sichuan-esque cuisine. While the décor isn't fancy, the thrice-cooked pork belly is white tablecloth-worthy. The chicken wing appetizer arrives under a blanket of whole chilies and the mapo tofu swims in a bath of dried shiitakes and peppery things. If you're a spice virgin, this is going to hurt; consider putting some booze lube between you and Mission Chinese.

ST. FRANCIS SODA FOUNTAIN
#NotAnOldDiner #breakfast
2801 24th Street

St. Francis is a pseudo-soda fountain with diner décor that serves updated diner breakfast, with many vegan items on the menu. There's a candy counter where they sell old-school candy like red vines and Pez dispensers if you need a sugar rush first thing in the morning. Seating is diner booths and swivel bar stools that may expose you to some man crack if you're not careful. Come here for vegan pancakes, tofu scrambles with pesto, vegan chorizo with hash, and huevos rancheros. Their potatoes are seasoned and have burnt, roasty ends, and the unlimited coffee can get dangerous.

TRULY MEDITERRANEAN
#FastLunch #shawarma #falafel
3109 16th Street

The guys behind the counter are stoned most of the time and the place is tiny, with little room to move around. But their shawarma and falafel are legit. Get a huge sandwich all wrapped up in lavash and sauced with tahini and spicy red sauce. The falafel combo platter comes with two dolmas, two sesame-crusted falafels with green parsley interiors, smoky baba ghanoush, oily but tasty hummus, onions liberally sprinkled with sumac, flavorful tabbouleh and perfectly diced cucumbers, and a side of slightly stale pita you can throw at birds. Seating is just a bar with stools (which are out of commission when there's a line inside) and a few plastic tables out on crazy-as-can-be 16th Street.

UDUPI PALACE
#dosas #IndianLunch
1007 Valencia Street

This palace has frosted glass chandeliers, street musician figurines on the walls, and it's filled with pungent (but not repulsive) Indian aromas and young, energetic Indian waiters. Prices are reasonable and lunch runs about $8–$10. Their long and chewy dosas are slightly crispy, come with various chutneys (ginger, tomato, coconut), and are stuffed with your choice of fillings. While the regular dosa is a monster of a thing, have a two-footer ($10.95) if you're looking to eat like royalty.

WEST OF PECOS
#TexMex #brunch
550 Valencia Street

As big as a Texas ranch, Pecos is covered in 150-year-old barn wood and decorated with bushels of chili peppers hanging from the ceiling. The dinner menu is a little Tex-Mex with some fancy American flair, where lobster sometimes finds its way into salads and enchiladas. Brunch has inventive but familiar dishes with bold flavors, like the Hatch Chile Burger, and is best paired with strong drinks like mezcal Bloody Marys. Even though the place can seat a stadium of Giants fans, there's normally a wait for brunch.

Wise Sons

WISE SONS DELICATESSEN
#JewishDeli #reuben
3150 24th Street

A modern Jewish deli right in the middle of the historic 24th Street district, Wise Sons serves all the right stuff. Upon entry, you'll see the big deli slicer and know that you're in for some good pastrami. Wise Sons makes a dressed-up reuben, where pastrami and corned beef mingle with kraut, cheese, and Russian dressing on rye. More pastrami? Get the pastrami fries with diced meaty chunks and gooey cheese sauce. For cold days, there is matzo ball soup, and for sugar cravings, the chocolate babka hits the spot. It's a little pricey and won't beat Manhattan delis, but worth a try when you've eaten everything in the Mission and just Mexi-can't.

YAMO
#Burmese #TrueStreetFood #CashOnly
3406 18th Street

Yamo is a real Burmese street food hole in the wall with flaming woks manned by tiny old ladies. Come in, place your order with the younger English-speaking girl, and get real close to others at the bar seating (room for two seats together max). Just about everything is $6 and you should get a few dishes, as the portions are small. While you wait, you'll see every ingredient being cut, cooked, or sprinkled from a giant plastic tub. Admire the noodle mounds being thrown in a wok at a moment's notice, and savor the feeling of being transported to a Burmese food stall, where flame-ups are part of the show.

Mission

The Mission's Mexican (and Latin) joints, with their burritos, tamales, tacos, and spicy salsas, are the best in the country. With a truckload to choose from, you can spend a month in the Mission and never have the same thing twice. This is just the tip of the super burrito.

STAND UP

LA TAQUERIA
2889 Mission Street

La Taqueria has been in the spotlight for a few years, making Food Network appearances and winning top accolades from burrito-tasting professionals. As such, this place is packed from the second the first tortilla is rolled out. Wade through the madness to get a carne asada super burrito. They don't do rice, which makes room for more meat.

PANCHO VILLA TAQUERIA
3071 16th Street

From 3 to 5 p.m., this fresh taco spot runs a happy hour where two of their tasty tacos are only $3! And these aren't some shit tacos, either; they're piled high with succulent meat. Doctor your tacos up at the expansive salsa bar in the back.

SIT-DOWN

EL METATE
2406 Bryant Street

A great place for a Mexican date, El Metate is done up with bright yellow tables, colorful décor, and a little salsa cart with wooden mariachi sculptures. While this is a sit-down joint, their authentic, delicious food doesn't break the bank.

Mexican

GRACIAS MADRE
2211 Mission Street

All vegan, all extra tasty—you'll need to put your name on a waiting list no matter when you come here. The décor is fancy and the front patio is the best seat in the house. Their tortillas come in a little basket and the guac is smooth. Get their huge Mojado Tamal, which comes slathered in tangy mole and cashew crema. All their veggies, especially the mushrooms, are roasted with care and the cocktail menu is small but good.

PAPALOTE MEXICAN GRILL
3409 24th Street

Order at the counter and sit down in their brightly painted dining room with paper dragons on the ceiling. A bowl of chips and salsa will arrive. Something about their mysteriously sweet, tangy, and spicy salsa will force your hand to reach for more chips.

Papalote's burritos are the fork and knife kind, especially the off-menu Triple Threat Burrito, a $20 monster that includes chicken, steak, and shrimp and was featured on *Throwdown! with Bobby Flay*. They've got tofu and soyrizo for veg heads and you can strip it down "naked" (over salad if you broke up with carbs.

STUMBLE IN DRUNK

EL FAROLITO
2779 Mission Street

Standing in the back of the 1 a.m. line at this super-popular joint seems daunting, but you'll be eating in no time. A guy runs down the line taking orders before you can even see the register. Commit to something quick (half chorizo and half carnitas super burrito it you're going at it like a pro), pay and moveover to the salsa bar to fill up on pickled jalapeños, flavorful verde, and pico. You'll only get through three-fourths of this burrito, but that will still feel like a big success.

TAQUERIA EL BUEN SABOR
697 Valencia Street

Buen Sabor hasn't been covered by some big newspaper or mag and is just fast, simple Mexican drunk food. Admire the weird palm tree painting and watch them cut fresh peppers, fry tortillas, and load up nachos with black beans, pico, sour cream, and cheese. Spicy salsa verde and roja sit on the table within arm's reach, and their carnitas burrito is juicy and smaller so you can actually finish it.

PANCHITA'S RESTAURANT NO. 2
3091 16th Street

This stretch of street is full of bars and you'll likely be drunk and hungry. Panchita's round little pupusas will satisfy all your fat and carb cravings. They stuff and grill them right on the sidewalk late nights so you can grab, eat, and keep the party moving.

TAQUERIA VALLARTA
3033 24th Street

A big blue-and-yellow cave with murals of Pancho Villa and friends and a toy grab machine in the corner, Vallarta smells insanely delicious, even when you're half sober first thing in the morning. The flattop behind the counter is always in flames, the salsa bar is packed with options (roasted pico and spicy habanero are the jam), and they have the biggest selection of vegetarian burritos in the Mission.

BONUS

TACOS EL PAISANO
Valencia Street and Cesar Chavez Street

A tiny truck in a car-wash parking lot, tucked behind the Salvation Army on Valencia, el Paisano feels like family. Try a tongue taco, grab a seat in their makeshift seating area, and enjoy the sounds of traffic whooshing by.

OTP Tip: For a sweet ending, hit up La Mejor Bakery by the 24th Street BART, where you can get a bag's worth of Mexican sweet breads for under $5, plus a free cookie for just being you.

👁 SEE AND DO

ASTERISK
#PopUpVenue #ArtGallery
3156 24th Street

We're big fans of local print publications and Asterisk puts together a magazine that's visually and mentally stimulating, covering food, fashion, culture, and politics around the city. This is their gallery space, decked out with beautiful wood finishes and lights, where they hold a variety of interesting events, pop-ups, and art shows. Stepping into Asterisk is a unique experience every time, and you can pick up a copy of their mag on your way out.

BLACK AND BLUE TATTOO
#InternationalStaff #Brucius
381 Guerrero Street

Idexa Stern is the lady who runs the show at Black and Blue. She's originally from Germany and employs an international staff that will help you figure out what you want in a handful of languages. Idexa herself has received recognition from the tattoo community for her geometric designs and steady hand. If you come here for something intricate, with fine lines, try to get an appointment with Brucius if he's around.

BODY MANIPULATIONS
3234 16th Street

Established in 1989, Body Manipulations is the oldest pro piercing studio in the country. A massive complex of everything you need to add a little pizzazz to your natural-born self, they have a wide assortment of jewelry displayed in the window like a gallery. They'll stretch your ears to fit those plugs, and are well versed in piercing the naughty bits. They also do some beautiful tattoo work for $180 an hour.

CLARION ALLEY
#StreetArt #AlwaysChanging

Between Mission and Valencia Streets (near 18th Street), lies an alley that's full of new and throwback art. Every garage door and wall is painted with low-rider graffiti and Chicano classics; these commingle with newer pieces that are both visually stimulating and political. The alley is perpetually morphing; every weekend new artists come in and leave their marks. Try to drop by the last weekend of October for the block party.

DÍA DE LOS MUERTOS (DAY OF THE DEAD)
#SkeletalParade #CommunityEvent

Once the raunchy raucousness of Halloween dies down, the Mission puts on a more somber—but quite spectacular—event to honor the dead. Outside of Mexico, this procession is the most elaborate Día de los Muertos display in North America. A parade of skeletal faces carrying burning sage and trucks loaded with musicians starts its journey up to Mission Street at 24th and Bryant Streets. With every step, the parade grows in volume and the spectacle is truly amazing. But this isn't just a tribute to the dead; political speakers will grab the attention of residents old and new to discuss issues (like gentrification) in an effort to maintain the homogeneity of this rich and colorful community.

OTP Tip: This isn't a drunk street party or an extension of slutty Halloween. Come here to observe respectfully—with or without face paint.

DOLORES PARK
#HillyPark #lounge #EatAndBeMerry
18th Street and Dolores Street

A spacious, hilly, green park between the Mission and the Castro, where people throw down a blanket, picnic, make out, spoon, tan, smoke weed, sell edibles, relax, and drink booze while watching the city from an elevated distance. There's a playground with ass-scorching metal slides, bikes, ice cream and beer vendors, dogs, and pet iguanas. People come here to just sit and wait for inevitable weird stuff to happen. Families with strollers know damn well to stay out of the middle party area and on the sideline slopes, so you never have to worry about accidentally killing a toddler with your secondhand smoke. The actual Mission Dolores (formally known as San Francisco de Asís) Church is close by, with many a street wanderer passed out on its glorious, historic steps.

OTP Tip: Brave the crazies just once at night to hike up to 20th and Church Streets at the far corner of the park to see some truly incredible lit-up views of the city. The Golden Fire Hydrant is up there, too.

GALERIA DE LA RAZA
#art #SugarSkulls
2857 24th Street

Mexican art and culture are on display at Galeria de la Raza, and the best time to stop by is around Día de los Muertos when the colorful sugar skulls make their way to the display window. Aside from the skulls, they hold exhibits year-round to showcase the best in Mexican art, from ancient forms to emerging artists. The space is big and open, and a nice way to get in touch with the community.

MISSION YOGA
#sweat #HippiePeople
2390 Mission Street

The owners of this studio (Juicy, Steve23, and their dog Pepper, who you'll see lounging on her queen pillow at the front desk) are passionate, incredibly dedicated people. It's all hippies, colors, and smiles until you hit the hot room of death and pain, kept at a true 105 degrees. The swirly sky-painted ceilings are low and the windows are covered with Mexi-colored fabric. After an intense class, you'll feel like you're on drugs and the rubber ducky collection in the bathroom will freak you the fuck out. Mission Yoga is a transformative place that'll kick your practice up to a new level if you let it.

THE ARMORY
#historic #kink
1800 Mission Street

A huge brick fortress built in 1912, the Armory spans almost an entire block. The inside of this building has seen it all. It was first used to hold army equipment, later turned into a sporting venue, used for a few scenes in *Star Wars*, and then remained vacant for some time until somebody realized it looked like the perfect sexy torture chamber. The current home of Kink.com (we know you've seen

at least one of their fine films), the quantity of chains, whips, and nipple clamps stored at the armory would make *Fifty Shades of Grey* turn red in the face. They hold tours, holiday parties, and special events. The Armory Club is their kinky bar across the street.

THE ROXIE THEATER
#OldestSFTheater #IndieFilms
3117 16th Street

The oldest operating cinema in the country (and the second oldest in the world), the Roxie has been a gathering place for indie film lovers since 1909 (and for porno fiends when it was a sexy house for a stint in the early '70s). It has changed hands among many nationalities that have passed through these parts and has premiered some of our favorite indie films throughout the years (like *Man Bites Dog*; see it). Currently, it stands as a duplex with forty-nine-seater Little Roxie two doors over. Admission is a modest $10.

YOU DON'T

Noe Valley borders the Mission and Castro neighborhoods and has a small-town vibe. Hidden away from the crowds up on the hill, it's like a nest for pregnant women, new moms, and the old people who love them. If you ever wander that far up the 24th Street hill, here is the best of what you'll find.

BEST BRUNCH

CHLOE'S CAFE
1399 Church Street

This place is a tiny cottage and it will feel impossible to get a seat with so many people clusterfucked together on the sidewalk. Shoot for an outdoor table and order the banana walnut pancakes, which come out warm, thick, and with a little nutty crunch. Their scrambles are perfection, especially with a bit of Jarlsberg cheese mixed in, and getting a mimosa to reward yourself for the wait is highly encouraged.

BEST CAFÉ

BERNIE'S
3966 24th Street

Bernie's may sound like a dive bar run by your drunk uncle, but it's a homey neighborhood coffee shop owned by a cool lady named Bernie. Decorated with iconic SF landmark photographs, it feels like a little cottage filled with amazing baked goods. It's heavy on moms and babies but has WiFi and bay window seating. Open earlier than you'll ever want coffee (5:30 a.m.). Try their specialty lattes and buttery oat jacks.

know Noe

BEST DINNER

SARU SUSHI BAR

3856 24th Street

This place is expensive, but good fish should not be cheap. Saru is a dark little spot, and the fish here is meticulously sourced (mostly from Japan) and served with flair. The tasting spoons ($6) are two chef-chosen spoons filled with a balanced, one-bite appetizer. While the sashimi omakase is a fantastic collection of the freshest fish in the world, go for the sushi tasting menu ($57) to get a little taste of their beautifully prepared rice. Don't leave room for dessert; blow it all on fish.

BEST DRINKS

CASKHOUSE

3853 24th Street

Given the demographic, Noe Valley isn't a big party spot, but the Caskhouse has pretty good pub food (sliders) and a decent beer selection. Come here for a few pints (the wine is overpriced), but don't expect a sloppy crowd. Your grandparents would drink here and complain about how loud everyone is talking, especially on game days.

BEST SHOP

CHOCOLATE COVERED (GIFTS & SWEETS)

4069 24th Street

Every inch of this shop is covered in dark navy-and-white tin boxes printed with vintage photographs of street sights, old high school emblems, baseball scenes, and historic landmarks. The empty spaces are filled with all kinds of chocolate in the form of bars, truffles, and sculptures. Even if you don't have a sweet tooth, this place is a visual trip and a wonderful place to purchase edible gifts.

SHOP

826 VALENCIA PIRATE SUPPLY STORE
#EyePatch #CoolDécor
826 Valencia Street

A gimmick for a good cause, the Pirate Supply Store sells kitschy items you might need to take on the high seas. Get your hand hooks, bottles of scurvy elixirs, whale feed, captain's logs, and, of course, eye patches. The store has a funky, not quite oceanlike, scent, an aquarium, and funny signs on the walls. While you can get real gifts, like pirate sea salt and pepper shakers, T-shirts, and wooden yo-yos, most things are just uselessly fun.

ALITE DESIGNS
#OutdoorGear #backpacks
3376 18th Street

The perfect modern backpacker store, Alite sells functional, minimalist, creatively designed outdoor gear. Camping gear, roll bags, water bottles, clips, and clasps hang on wooden racks and walls around this clean, well-curated store. One of the standout items is the bootlegger ($200), a backpack with interchangeable accessories based on your needs. Tiny Warrior is a little coffee shop tucked right in the corner that specializes in iced coffee ($5), the best of which is the Vietnamese, where they use burnt caramel syrup that they can serve with chocolate ice cubes (plus $2), making everything extra fudgey. It's going to be stupid expensive, but it's worth a try.

AQUARIUS RECORDS
#GoodVinyl #arcades
1055 Valencia Street

One of the best record stores in the Bay Area, Aquarius leaves out all the riffraff and stocks the store with the weird, funky stuff that'll make you a hit at all the record-listening parties. Whether you're a DJ, a wannabe music connoisseur, or just a lover of nostalgic music formats, they'll help you navigate the murky music waters. There are also old-school arcades around the store if you can't tell a record from a horseshoe.

BORDERLANDS BOOKS
#coffee #books #SciFi
866 Valencia Street

A split space that's half café and half bookstore, Borderlands serves De La Paz coffee and sells lots of nerdy books. The café is set up like an extended living room with an armoire, a mag stand in the middle, two super-comfy armchairs, redwood tables, and viney plants winding all around the place. It's clean and bright. The baristas are older hippie, book lover types, rather than your regular bearded espresso men. The bookstore part is organized by genre with a SciFi focus and rare books under the glass counter. You can browse the bookstore, buy something to read, get a pastry, and read in music-less silence.

CHROME
#MessengerBags #SewOnSite
962 Valencia Street

If you don't want to risk your life delivering a manila envelope but want to look like you do, hook yourself up with a Chrome messenger bag from their ever-changing lineup. This hub location has a sewing station where you can watch them make custom bags on-site.

OTP Tip: Chrome also has a SOMA location, where you can get your bags with a side of Four Barrel coffee at the adjacent mini-café.

DIJITAL FIX
#headphones #boomboxes #CoolDesigns
820 Valencia Street

A crafty store focused on the art of sound, with various electronics, expensive headphones, and a lounge chair decked out in speakers. In addition to the modern stuff, they also carry some old boom boxes, hokey electronics, amps, turntables, and random items of interest. It's fun to come in here to see what kind of crazy designs people come up with to remix audio gear.

DOG EARED BOOKS
#FreeBooks #CoolMags
900 Valencia Street

An older bookstore in a bright corner spot that gets good light with a box of free books up front. Their shelves are tall and well stocked with a variety of titles, and they carry cool magazines. They also sell journals, notebooks, and postcards, many with prints done by local artists. The staff leaves you alone so you can browse for hours with nobody hovering near your headspace.

LUZ DE LUNA
#BetterGifts #DayOfTheDead
3182 24th Street

Right by the 24th Street BART, Luz de Luna is a little intimidating to go in at first, but once inside you'll be in a paradise of Mexican gifts, art, and jewelry. Luz de Luna carries distinctive items (none of those Lucha Libre masks) that'll make thoughtful gifts for your unlucky friends who couldn't see this beautiful part of the Mission for themselves. Around Día de los Muertos, the store gets all dolled up in skulls, flowers, and somber celebratory goods.

MISSION SKATEBOARD
#boards #SkateKids
3045 24th Street

A local skate shop that'll hook you up with a board or the parts you need to make yours functional again. Everyone who works here is helpful and friendly. Come on a weekend to have your old skater heart warmed by the ten-year-old kids hanging out front, just discovering the magic of skating and teaching each other the ropes.

MISSION THRIFT
#BurningManCentral #FunLabels
2330 24th Street

An expansive store full of all kinds of crazy shit, most of which is suitable for destroying at the Playa during Burning Man. They've got the requisite desert goggles and weird-ass hats, DIY freak gear, boas, bell bottoms, and polyester at really low prices. A good aimless dig is made easier by labeled categories like "sparkly tops" and "pirate wench" tabbed around the many racks.

NO SHOP
#vintage #SaleRack
389 Valencia Street

There are a lot of vintage gems here from the '70s, '80s, and '90s. Go here to pick through crop tops, dresses, rompers, coats, and high-waisted jeans. This shop is big on men's flannel and carries leather boots for both sexes. You can have it all for about $15–$30 per piece, and there's also a good selection of sale items on the front rack that runs from $8 to $10. The nondescript electronica playing will get you in the mood for weird, and if you pick around some you'll find a good piece to add to your wardrobe.

PAINTED BIRD
#SassyVintage #silver #LeatherBoots
1360 Valencia Street

The shop is small but very well curated. Here, whether it's H&M or Helmut Lang, you'll find items that are on-trend and some that are just quirky enough to make you rethink your style. They've got kimonos, vintage dresses, lots of Navajo flair, an extensive selection of affordable, worn-in leather boots, and a few accessories carefully placed around the store. The counter girl is never up in your shopping business and most things cost around $25. They've got two racks for men and silver jewelry ($25–$100) at the counter.

PAXTON GATE
#taxidermy #CactusGarden
824 Valencia Street

A touristy store of curiosities, our Paxton favorites include turkey toes, deer ribs, shark jaws, and a box of old bones and teeth for sale at reasonable prices ($2–$20). The whole store feels like a terrarium filled with taxidermy and medical anatomy books. There's also a cactus garden out back to take a breather from the displays of the dead.

THE FIZZARY
#AdultCandyStore #SodaPop
2949 Mission Street

Fully stocked with every bubbly soda in the universe, the Fizzary is a naughty place where you can joyfully purchase fizzy drinks without a care in the world. This isn't Coke or Sprite, but specialty crafted adult sodas devoid of corn syrup and other bullshit. There's a wall of sodas like Buckin' Root Beer from Jackson Hole, Canadian cream soda, chai cola from Taylor's Tonics, and a truckload more. You can buy them by the bottle,

or fill a fold-out four pack with three sodas ($2 each) and get the fourth one free. Some times they even throw in a piece of taffy.

THE WOODS
#curiosities #HologramPostcards
3248 16th Street

A morbid little shop of curiosities. Deep in The Woods you'll find lots of creepy cake toppers, eerie vintage photographs, and portraits of old men with ants crawling on their heads. One of our coolest finds were hologram postcards ($4) of bats, horses, elephants, and running dogs sold with mechanized easel stands that display their full range of motion and create the visual illusion of movement. Next door there's more jewelry, caterpillar and cockroach birthday cards, and creepy knickknacks. Owned by two lovely sisters (Lisa and Sandy Wood), this place is their collage of strange but beautiful things, meant to stir up feelings of intrigue.

PARTYING

500 CLUB
#dive #OpenForBreakfastBeers
500 Guerrero Street

500 opens at 6 a.m., and given that it's dark and cavernous already you don't even have to feel like you've left your bed to down a beer before sunrise. Their daytime bartender is a large, towering man who'll make you feel safe when he gets you piss-drunk way too early in the day. 500 is divey, charming, and better than a bowl of Frosted Flakes.

ABV
#kimchi #cocktails
3174 16th Street

ABV (alcohol by volume) is a cocktail bar that does bar food fusion right. We don't know about you, but we'll eat anything with kimchi on it, and ABV has a kimchi fritter ($8)—a pancake covered in kimchi and bonito

flakes—that hits all those salty fermented notes your mouth is after. ABV doesn't play by any sort of rules and will fuse whatever's clever, like chicken pot pie empanadas or falafel corn dogs. This creativity also applies to their cocktails, which are unexpected combinations of fresh ingredients, booze, and spices. ABV is run by some big names in the culinary and mixology scenes, and they blend their talents seamlessly at this super-popular food-centric bar with four Fernets on tap.

AMNESIA
#beer #wine #music
853 Valencia Street

Amnesia is a laid-back spot to catch an indie show just about any night of the week. The space itself is large and dark with a legit stage set up deep in the back. It's a casual bar where you can grab a glass of wine or beer, cozy up in one of their booths, and let the music move you. Shows are mostly free (or max $5), and they put on acoustic acts (like gypsy jazz and bluegrass) but will mix it up with open mics, comedy night, and monthly dance parties, too.

BENDER'S BAR & GRILL
#SundayBBQ #BestKindOfDive
806 South Van Ness Avenue

Bender's is only slightly *Futurama*-themed, and is a comfortable neighborhood bar with perks. There are bike racks right in the middle of the bar (and helmet shelves at the entrance), an elevated pool table, and a side room with "Hail Seitan," a flaming chrome kitchen specializing in vegan bar food. Bender's draws you into its hole of cold chillin' every night of the week with deals like Ass-Fnd Happy Hour, where drink prices are slashed again from 11 p.m. to 2 a.m. on Mondays; Whiskey Wednesdays, where it's $5 for a PBR plus shot of whiskey; and a free BBQ on Sunday out back. From the Leather Tongue logo mural and the fake IDs plastered onto their tables, Bender's does dive décor well.

BLIND CAT
#DiveBar #CashOnly
3050 24th Street

Blind Cat is a neighborhood dive that does not take itself too seriously and attracts a crowd with a similar mind-set. It's a little smelly, kind of grimy, with random music and ridiculous wall art. There's a pool table, they pour their drinks the way you would at home, and nobody cares if you're loud and offensive.

DALVA
#sexy #SecretCocktailLounge
3121 16th Street

The main bar is long, dark, packed at 8 p.m., and always playing something weird on the projector. There's a semisecret cocktail lounge in the back, called the "Hideout," that's small but stylish, decked out in tiny taxidermied woodland creatures. Get whatever the special is on the side chalkboard or play it safe with the smoking gun ($12), a smoky concoction of bourbon and three bitters. There is a sea of couples, but if your game is good you can snatch a single someone from the front, bring her back for a cocktail, and then head upstairs for more secluded seating.

DELIRIUM
#shitshow #pool
3139 16th Street

A corner bar that's always surrounded by drunks smoking cigs outside and talking shit. If there's a game on at Delirium, expect to clap in unison just to fit in. There's a pool table and arcade in the back, but most of the action centers around the booze-dispensing bar in the middle. Delirium gets real sloppy quickly and is so narrow and crowded that you're bound to make new wasted friends with every visit.

DOC'S CLOCK
#dive #shuffleboard #pinball
2575 Mission Street

What time is it? It's cocktail o'clock! Doc's doesn't do fancy, but when you're looking for strong and cheap ($3 well drinks), this place hits the spot. Once you're good and cocktailed, try your shaky hand at shuffleboard (with PBR pucks), Pac-Man, or *Pirates*

of the Caribbean pinball. There's always something weird on the projector screen and a fun crowd to shoot the shit with.

ELBO ROOM
#legendary #LiveMusic
647 Valencia Street

Around since 1935, Elbo Room is in danger of being turned into a condo, so if you're reading this and it's still there, you must go before the Google geeks move in. A multi-purpose bar and venue, Elbo Room is like a big cave of fun with vested bartenders, $5–$6 mixed drinks, a pinball room, and pretend psychic readings on the back couch. On most nights, they also host various musicians in their side room, which has a small cover but always offers a good time.

ELIXIR
#historic #bourbon
3200 16th Street

One of the oldest bars in San Francisco, Elixir looks intimidating from the outside, but once you get past the guido James Dean look-alike, you'll realize that it's just a plain ol' regular bar with a lot of dark liquor. The crowd seems to ebb and flow and is a little older. This isn't our favorite place to hang, but for the history it's good to pop in for some firewater, then venture on.

EL TECHO DE LOLINDA
#RooftopBar #FeelsSwank
2518 Mission Street

You will walk by a guy sitting at a host stand at the ground level and think that it's probably too fancy for your blood. But it's not. All you do is tell him you're going to the roof and he'll direct you to the PH floor. The elevator doors open into a warmed roof patio with strings of lights and a gorgeous view of the whole Mission. The communal tables are for drinks (sit and they'll get your order); the square tables are for food. Their cocktails are a little weak, but the high-above-the-Mission atmosphere is a unique way to escape the crowded streets down below.

LATIN AMERICAN CLUB
#SalsaDancing #piñatas
3286 22nd Street

Walk in under the faded sign hanging way too high to be seen, and you'll be impressed by Latin American Club's spacious, slightly dank interior with dusty piñatas hanging in clusters overhead. Run by a friendly non-Latina, this place is filled with eclectic things like sparkly vinyl booths, mismatched bistro tables, a giant wooden cut-out of a hamster leaning on the wall, and exactly twelve cuckoo clocks. If you order a margarita, know that you will not leave with the same sturdy legs that got you there.

LONE PALM
#EgyptInTheMission
#AfterWorkHangout
3394 22nd Street

With an Egypt-meets-Mission feel, Lone Palm is where local service industry peeps go to unwind after work. That cute waiter who served you brunch will be mingling with your barista from this morning. Everyone seems to know each other, but it's not cliquey and the drinks are strong enough to get you talkin' shop, too.

MAKE-OUT ROOM
#dance #LiveMusic #typewriters

3225 22nd Street

This place is strange and has never-ending New Year's ceiling décor. They put on a lot of different music shows, which vary in both genre and quality. The first Monday of the month is Attack of the Typewriters, where they pull out the vintage ink keys and encourage you to write to local politicians while they feed you booze.

OTP Tip: If there's a guy in here hitting one note on the Caslo, get the fuck out before your ears bleed.

MONK'S KETTLE
#CraftBeers #FoodPairings

3141 16th Street

Named for old Belgian monks who brewed their beer in kettles, this is a place for people who like to get a little fancy about beer, food, and pairing the two. There will be a wait, but once you finally squeeze into Monk's Kettle you'll understand the crowds. The beer menu is the length of a master's thesis and has some hard-to-find craft brews that pair perfectly with their food menu. Their malty hop salt fries work with what-

ever beer you get, but for bigger appetites and broader palates, use the servers as a resource to help you pair every bite with a beer.

PUBLIC WORKS
#club #dance #drugs

161 Erie Street

With a $20 cover, this place is all about that good EDM music and draws an eclectic crowd of house lovers. It's a smaller warehouse space with two rooms, a big dance floor and stage downstairs, and a loungier upstairs (with a strange cabinet in the middle). There are no creepers grinding on your butt, they put on a stimulating light show, and while there aren't many wallflowers, if you need a breather, a few bleachers are set up on the main level. They're open until 4 a.m., people do drugs, and there's an outdoor area for smokers and a requisite bacon-wrapped hot dog stand on the corner.

RADIO HABANA SOCIAL CLUB
#LotsOfFlair #tiny #sangria

1109 Valencia Street

This place is closet-small and you'll need some cojones to wade through all the hanging flair at the entrance, elbow-shove your way between a couple of old Latin dudes,

and negotiate your body into a seat. But if you're successful, the payoff is stupendous. Radio Habana Social Club is the kind of place you go to gather the wildest stories you've ever heard and relay them to your vanilla friends. Come here for live music, sit back with a sangria ($6 for a large), and let the weirdness in.

REVOLUTION CAFE
#SidewalkCafé #LiveMusic
3248 22nd Street

A small, open space that mostly spills onto the sidewalk, Revolution is equal parts coffee shop, wine bar, and live music venue that features the indie-est of performers. We're not sure they prescreen all the acts they book, but for the small investment of a cup of coffee or a glass of wine, you can see somebody sing their heart out most nights of the week.

SHOTWELL'S
#AllAboutBeer #NeighborhoodBar
3349 20th Street

With its old-timey décor and thick, wood bar, Shotwell's feels stout (and serves it on tap, along with many other beers). Naming themselves after their cross street got them big brownie points with the neighbors who frequent this spot. There's a pool table and pinball for a little friendly competition. Shotwell's has a warm vibe, attracts good company, and serves terrific beer (but no liquor).

SOUTHERN PACIFIC BREWING
#brewery #FancyFood #AirplaneHangar
620 Treat Avenue

What's it like to down beers in an airplane hangar? Hit up Southern Pacific to find out. While you won't find a 747 parked here, you do get a feel for how massive a place

needs to be to house airplanes. Get the pork belly–topped mac and cheese, plus a flight of house beers served in tiny cups, and you'll be ready for takeoff.

THE CHAPEL
#MusicVenue #BigNames #OldMortuary
777 Valencia Street

Don't come here to drink unless it's happy hour; do come here to see some bigger performers like Fiona Apple, Fleet Foxes, and James Blake. The Chapel used to be a mortuary and has immaculate wooden vaulted ceilings and beautiful lighting. While it does have several divided areas, it's still a pretty intimate venue with balanced acoustics and reasonable ticket prices ($15–$35).

OTP Tip: The Vestry next door does a decent, Creole-centric bottomless brunch.

THE HOMESTEAD
#peanuts #dogs #weeknights
2301 Folsom Street

Some of the best bars in the world are covered in peanut shells and you can add the Homestead to that list. On any given weekday, there are a handful of dogs hanging out, lots of beers on tap, and a bunch of friendly beer drunks. It's just a simple square bar where you can litter, hit on the bartenders, and pet pooches.

TIN TAN
#MexicanDive #BlaringMexicanTunes
3065 16th Street

This place probably sees a non-Mexican once every lunar eclipse and that's what makes it fantastic. Even if you speak perfect Spanish, if your face is unfamiliar, everyone at Tin Tan will just pretend they don't understand you. Every beer on tap is flat and served by a Mexican lady wearing hoop earrings. The pool tables are always packed with mamacitas pounding balls, the music is ranchero on blast, and there's an out-of-place Marvel versus Capcom arcade up front.

OTP Tip: Don't fuck up going to the bathroom: A key with an unruly metal attachment is hidden in a drawer in the back, and you have to awkwardly ask one of the dudes sitting back there watching soccer for it.

TRICK DOG
#WorldFamous #cocktails #AmazingBarFood
3010 20th Street

In 2014, Trick Dog was named one of the best bars in the world by a prestigious group of global drinkers who put out a top 50 list every year. What makes it so great? Their drink menu is crafted around a fun theme and changes every six months. When we visited, each of their drinks was based on an SF neighborhood. While we were afraid to find out what the Castro tasted like, Trick Dog assured us there wouldn't be ground-up feather boas or leather butt plugs anywhere near our drinks. As for the food, their thrice-cooked fries, manimal-style, rip In-N-Out's version to shreds. Given their recent bump in popularity, we expect the crowd to get douchier. For now, Trick Dog's got us on a short leash.

ZEITGEIST
#DiveBar #BestBackyard
199 Valencia Street

Zeitgeist is run by a bunch of old punks. Your first hurdle here is the doorman who's usually a weird mix of angry and funny, with a heavy layer of drunk on top. Next up, the bartenders don't always make nice, but it's expected for this kind of place. Your goal here is to order a bunch of beer and get your ass out in the backyard, a huge space with a trailer park feel. Smoke whatever you want, despite what the signs say, and refill your beer often. It's best to start drinking midday for a hit of vitamin D before the sun goes down. There are many bathrooms but zero mirrors, which may be a good thing.

FUN FACT
The tamale lady is a legend, known for appearing out of the drunk darkness to feed the Mission masses little pregnant cornhusks stuffed with masa and meat. You've gotta believe in the tamale lady and she will come.

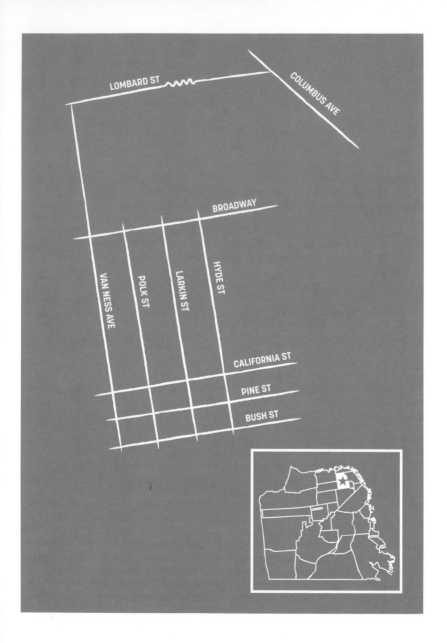

NOB HILL/

RUSSIAN HILL

Nob Hill and Russian Hill are what you picture when you think of residential San Francisco, complete with rich, manicured ladies walking their groomed dogs, popping into salons, bakeries, and cafés as cable cars roll by in the background. Except every now and again, a crazy person will stagger out from some random corner. Polk Street is the main drag and where you'll find Swan Oyster Depot's super-fresh seafood, cool bars, both old (Shanghai Kelly's) and new (Tonic), and Bob's Donut & Pastry Shop, a 24-hour, old-school doughnut shop. The main tourist attraction here is crooked-ass Lombard Street, which you should see with sober eyes.

COFFEE AND BAKERIES

ANOTHER CAFE

#CoolDécor #AtticSeating
1191 Pine Street

A corner double-decker café at the top of a hill, this isn't just another café. They've got smooth espresso, pastries, four beers on tap, and smiley service. Another Cafe has interesting décor with creepy-cute, sinister bunnies painted on skateboard decks lining the walls, and the art extends to the bathroom, which is covered with a black-and-white mural. Once named a top place to get work done by Foursquare, the café draws a mixed crowd of old people and laptoppers. While the downstairs seating is spacious, the attic upstairs is not built for anyone over six feet tall.

BATTER BAKERY

#BakedGoods #LunchByThePound
#CookieHappyHour
2127 Polk Street

As you enter Batter, you will be bombarded by an array of packaged cookies and baked goods until your eyes fall onto a counter packed with more choices. They've got cakes, bars, ridiculous cupcakes, and fantastic lunch food, like hearty grain salads, polenta sticks, brisket, and turkey meat loaf by the pound. They brew Sightglass coffee by the cup and best seats are up front by the window for prime people watching.

OTP Tip: Come for cookie happy hour when all cookies are $2 from 3 to 6 p.m. daily.

Batter Bakery

BOB'S DONUT AND PASTRY SHOP

#GiantDoughnuts #24Hours
#DrunkFood
1621 Polk Street

At one of the few places in SF that's open 24/7, Bob has been stuffing his doughnuts into the mouths of bad-decision makers since the '60s. They don't mess with the classic flavors, but they do offer a giant doughnut that can double as an airplane neck pillow. The freshest doughnuts are made late-night, and their apple fritters are legendary.

CONTRABAND COFFEE BAR

#coffee #UniquePastries
1415 Larkin Street

Tucked away on a residential street, Contraband smuggles in the good, strong brew. You can have your coffee prepared in a number of ways, from pour-overs to chemex, and they sell some interesting pastries, like pistachio croissants. The décor is all red and black with communal laptop seating, window stools that let your feet dangle, and chairs on the sidewalk that are perfect for watching the California Street cable car roll by.

FLOUR & CO

#StumptownCoffee #MonkeyBread
#cornbread
1030 Hyde Street

A bakery that serves Stumptown coffee and has small but creative and rich pastries, Flour & Co offers individual servings of pull-apart monkey bread, brown butter cookies, and sandwiches held together by cornbread. Flour & Co is also known for their breakfast sandwiches on pretzel bread and spicy chai lattes. The inside seating is awkward, so sit outside on the slope of Hyde Street and eat your fancy pastries with one pinky in the air.

SAINT FRANK COFFEE

#FancyCoffee #CustomEspressoMachine
2340 Polk Street

If you really want to get into the fancy swing of things in this bougie neighborhood without throwing down too many bills, Saint Frank is the place to do it. All white and wood, it feels as sterile as feet that don't smell, but the coffee is undeniably great. Their espresso machine was custom-built for the shop and looks like it came from outer space. It's a bit of a fashion show, and their specialty lattes will make you feel like a pampered poodle.

 EAT

ALIMENT

#AmericanMenu #TreatYourself
#DateNight
786 Bush Street

Aliment is a clean and modern restaurant with minimalist décor and a streamlined new American menu that changes frequently. The mainstay is their fried Brussels sprouts app ($9), a simple dish with complex flavors imparted by a caramel of fish sauce and nori. Each item on their menu is carefully thought out, pairing proteins with interesting ingredients and punchy sauces. Aliment is a romantic date spot and has a wide selection of wine.

MILLER'S EAST COAST DELI

#BigFatReuben #knishes
1725 Polk Street

Using the words *East Coast* when naming your deli is a ballsy move in the West, but Miller's backs it up big-time. Conjuring up the Lower East Side Jewish deli gods, Miller's creates big-ass reubens packed with enough corned beef to break your jaw. To do it right, get it on rye with kraut and a little Russian dressing. They also have knishes, latkes, bagels with lox and—oddly—pizza. We judge a good deli by its pickle, and Miller's is a winner.

MYMY COFFEE SHOP

#brunch #SouffléPancakes
#BreakfastBurgers
1500 California Street

The popular brunch spot in this neighborhood, MyMy(my!) their food is delicious. You ever have a soufflé pancake? Two different

things, you say? Not at MyMy. They take the goodness of a light, fluffy soufflé and somehow transform it into the best pancakes you've ever had. For something meatier, they offer a number of burgers, and the MOT burger with its heavenly sausage patty, is the big standout. This place is tiny, and you'll have to wait your turn (at least thirty to forty minutes) on the weekends.

NARA SUSHI

#fresh #LunchSpecial
1515 Polk Street

This place serves quality fish for the price, especially during happy hour (weekdays, 3 to 6 p.m.) where sashimi is $1 a piece and sake is only $2. Go for something simple to start and then treat yourself to a wacky

swamp roll, a bold contrast of flavors where well-seasoned seaweed salad is thrown atop a tuna roll. Nara has solid lunch specials and you get a feast of five nigiri, a California roll, salad, and miso soup for under $10.

NICK'S CRISPY TACOS
#FishTacos #GiantClub
1500 Broadway

Big and intimidating, like a giant super club, Nick's doesn't seem like a taco place. Enter through the side door during the day and you'll find the giant is sitting there empty, free for the crispy taco eating. The pescado taco, done up "Nick's way"—where for 95 cents more you get a heaping serving of cheese and guac over top—is the way to go. Come here for $5 taco feasts on Friday, stay for the two coronas for $6 deal, and leave before it turns into douchey nightclub Rouge.

NOB HILL CAFE
#gnocchi #pizza
1152 Taylor Street

A solid place for meaty, cheesy Italian, Nob Hill Cafe is casual and priced just right. You can't go wrong with their pillowy gnocchi ($14.95), bathed in a rich sausage and beef Bolognese. Their special pizzas are always fantastic, and their wine list is short and to

the point, with glasses running about $8–$10 each. It's not the most romantic place, but when a hearty carb craving hits, this little café's got you covered.

SWAN OYSTER DEPOT
#FreshOysters #FamousFood
#TreatYourself
1517 Polk Street

Swan Oyster Depot is the epitome of fresh-from-the-bay seafood. You can see the daily offerings on ice up front, and you'll be up there for a good hour before anything gets into your mouth. Once inside, the seating is counter-only and the prices are steep. You'll want everything, but can reasonably afford enough to be comfortably full. The clams and oysters will breathe their last salty breath just moments before hitting your plate, their composed salads always come with fresh slivers of seafood, and the live uni ($18), hacked open in front of your eyes, is a must.

Chef's Tasting Menus

San Francisco is a tasting menu destination city, and a large concentration of the city's finest dining is in this neighborhood. We can't afford them, but fuck, don't they sound tasty?

GARY DANKO

800 North Point Street
$114, five courses; $85 wine pairing

While it's the biggest name when it comes to fine dining, some say Gary Danko is a bit dated. Nonetheless, people line up two months in advance to try his menu, laced with buttery lobster, lots of caviar, and perfectly cooked risotto.

LA FOLIE

2316 Polk Street
$140, seven courses ($105 vegetarian, five courses); $80 wine pairing

A husband-and-wife team serve fancy French fare at La Folie. This place is where couples celebrate their important dates by throwing down a wad of cash on a feast of seasonal vegetables, succulent meats, and well-developed sauces.

ACQUERELLO

1722 Sacramento Street
$95, three courses; $120, four courses; $140, five courses; $100 wine pairing

Holding onto two Michelin stars, Acquerello is an Italian spot that's been at it for over twenty-five years. To keep their menu fresh, they constantly explore new cooking techniques and flavor combinations (like tempura mussels!). When truffle season hits, Acquerello offers a white-truffle tasting menu that will run you a cool $395 per person.

Grandma left you a fortune? Take us with you to one of these joints. We promise to behave.

◉ SEE AND DO

CABLE CAR MUSEUM AND CAR BARN

#free #CableCarControlCenter
1201 Mason Street

Dedicated to the history of SF's iconic form of transportation, the Cable Car Museum is filled with artifacts like old tokens, streetlights, and photographs. Just when you think everything in here is an ancient relic, you'll enter a room with giant turning wheels and cables, and you'll learn that this is the mechanism behind the cable car you came in on. Entrance is free and the place will take less than an hour to explore. To get there, take either the Powell-Hyde or the Powell-Mason cable car, which both stop right outside the museum.

GRACE CATHEDRAL

#free #LightRibbons
1100 California Street

You don't have to be a Jesus freak to appreciate the beauty of this towering, French gothic cathedral. Inside, you'll find a lot of beautiful things. There are colorful ribbons hanging from the impossibly high ceiling over the main altar that mimic rays of light that shine through the church's stained-glass windows. The floors of the indoor labyrinth are carefully patterned in dizzying circles, and the entire church will fill you with awe. You can just walk in during operating hours or take an organized tour for $25.

LOMBARD STREET

#TouristAttraction #WindyStreet
1000–1099 Lombard Street

The world's most crooked road, Lombard looks more like the *Price Is Right* plinko game than an actual street. It's a brick paved road with eight hairpin turns slanted at a puke-inducing 27 degrees. If you came to SF in a car, park it and hike up to the top instead. Along the hike, you can watch tourists wiggle their way around while you enjoy the beautiful flowerbeds that line this ridiculous stretch of street.

SHOP

BELLE COSE/MOLTE COSE

#men #women #BricABrac
2036–2044 Polk Street

This place is a side-by-side women's and men's boutique that's designed to look much more expensive than it really is. The women's side offers more "sophisticated" fashions, with a little blurb on each rack about the local designer who created the pieces. The jewelry, glasses, and other accessories are a good mix of new and vintage, and the sale racks have items that range from $40 to $60. The mostly men's side has SF relics (like firefighter helmets), new T-shirts, wall art, and a whole display of cuff links and vintage tie pins, along with random housewares, flasks, socks, and typewriters. There's also a small baby store, but we wouldn't dare go in.

RELOVE VINTAGE & MODERN RESALE

#vintage #designer #AlwaysFashionable
1815 Polk Street

ReLove is a husband-and-wife shop, where the lady does all the merchandising and really knows what's up when it comes to fashion. While items here are from different eras, designers, and shitty corporate stores alike, each piece is stylish and wearable. From Cavalli to Free People, down to Uniqlo and H&M, the owner doesn't care if it's $2,000 or $10, as long as it's sassy. You'll find vintage T-shirts, crop tops, dresses from all eras, leather vests and jackets, studded shorts, worn-in jeans, and a wide selection of shoes and silver. The inventory changes with the seasons and there's a store dog to keep an eye on things.

PARTYING

BIMBO'S 365 CLUB

#HistoricVenue #CoolDécor
1025 Columbus Avenue

Established in 1931, Bimbo's feels like the kind of place the Sopranos would go for some live entertainment. There's a bit of an old Vegas nightclub vibe, with statues in the lobby, velvety carpeting, and red lights. While Bimbo's used to be all showgirls and big instrumental bands, it now hosts artists like the Raconteurs and Jill Scott. They put on comedy variety shows, holiday parties, and private events.

HOPWATER DISTRIBUTION

#JustBeer #CoolDécor
850 Bush Street

A sleek, brick house of beer with just an "H" logo on the window, Hopwater has the slickest beer taps. Instead of your average beer handles, they've got unlabeled spouts marked only with numbers across the back wall of the bar. Hopwater only serves beer (and food), and their selection rotates frequently. This place draws a mixed crowd and feels like a minimalist version of a beer garden without the sloppy drunks.

KOZY KAR

#WaterBed #porn
1548 Polk Street

People definitely have sex here, and if your standards aren't high, you can, too. Kozy Kar has grimy waterbeds, car booths that play videos with porn spliced in, and playboys découpaged all over the bathroom floor. Shag carpet? Check. Kozy up to this bar and just try to leave without feeling all kinds of dirty.

LA TRAPPE

#MonkBeer #BeerFood
800 Greenwich Street

La Trappe is all about Belgian beers and serves them in appropriate glassware. Their selection is huge, with rare finds from Trappist breweries, and they always have something good on tap. They're so big on beer that they stick it into the food menu wherever possible, serving beer-steeped stews and huge portions of mussels with beer-spiked broth. The atmosphere is appropriately that of a Belgian monk's basement and the crowd skews older.

SHANGHAI KELLY'S

#Steelers #GoldRushCriminalHangout
2064 Polk Street

A sports dive for young and old bros alike, Kelly's is a packed-with-crap corner spot that's always loud and lively. It may be miles from Pittsburgh, but this bar roots for the Steelers, and when there isn't a game on, people just get Irish drunk and scream for the fuck of it. Named after the "King of Crimps," an Irishman from the Gold Rush era who earned his criminal gold stars by being the best sailor hitman around, this is a great place to get shanghaied and see if you live to tell the tale.

SODA POPINSKI'S

#Nintendo #WheelOfMisfortune
1548 California Street

Haphazardly Russian-themed, Soda Popinski's brings out the inner kid in you and then feeds him enough booze to get him grounded for life. We never really thought about playing Nintendo drunk, but turns out it's an excellent idea. Two-for-one happy hour really gets you lubed up for stomping

on turtles and popping into pipes. If you like to gamble for your drinks, they've got a wheel of misfortune where it's $10 per spin and you're guaranteed a drink, which ranges from picklebacks to entire bottles of champagne.

OTP Tip: Aim that wheel pin toward the Mule Kick, a $22 Moscovian concoction served in a boot.

THE BUCCANEER

#dive #fireplace
2155 Polk Street

The Buccaneer is a warm, sometimes sweaty, bar with a designated pool area in the back and a fireplace. The bartenders here are friendly and attentive no matter who stumbles in. They've got better beers on tap than most dives, which includes Chimay and Boddington's (for $3.50!). The Bucc is as divey as Russian Hill can get without losing face.

THE HYDE OUT

#UpstairsLounge #LocalsBar
1068 Hyde Street

A neighborhood bar that attracts an interesting crowd of regulars young and old, the Hyde Out has one of the best views in Nob Hill. Grab a beer and head upstairs where floor-to-ceiling windows give you a perched view of the surrounding neighborhood. You'll likely get chatty with locals, maybe take a shot or two, and feel like you live there, too.

Tonic

TONIC

#FishBowl #greyhound
2360 Polk Street

If you're traveling with a group of four or more and need a fast, weird way to get fucked up, Tonic serves a ridiculous fishbowl for $23. Each mini-aquarium contains about fifteen shots of vodka and rum, some other sugary shit, and Swedish fish (yeah, the candy). This thing is so sweet and potent that you will need nothing but a barf bag for the rest of the night. If you're not looking to pass out, Tonic also makes an excellent greyhound with fresh grapefruit juice.

WOODS POLK STATION

#BeerForBreakfast #empanadas
2255 Polk Street

Any place that has special breakfast beers is fine by us. This place is like a casual café where coffee is swapped out for beer and croissants for empanadas (from El Porteño). Their beers are always creative, with an entire line of Yerba Mate-infused brews, and the bartenders are barista-chatty. The space is tiny, with a little service station in the middle. WOODS also does beer flights where you get four decent pours for $10.

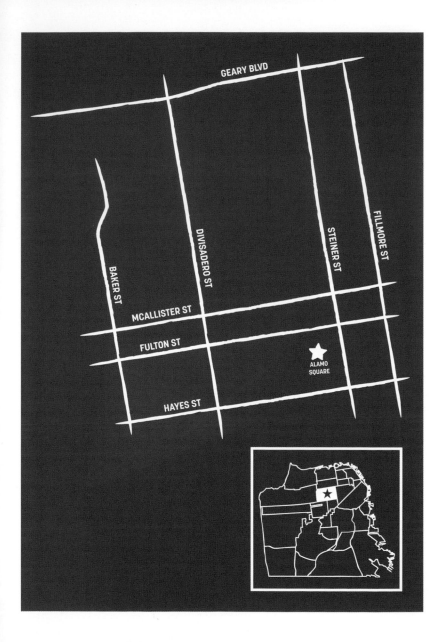

NOPA

NOPA (North of Panhandle) is the realtor-fabricated name for the combination of Alamo Square, the Panhandle, and Western Addition (which includes the jazzy Fillmore district). And while entitled newcomers have blindly embraced the acronym, others pull the bullshit card every time they hear the name. The namesake restaurant, NOPA, with its eternity-long waits, month-ahead reservations, and arm-and-leg prices, really sealed the fate of this hood. But we found a few ruffs among these overpriced diamonds. Plus, what this new NOPA lacks in cheap restaurants, it makes up for in dive bars (like Madrone) and music venues (like the Independent). Liquid lunch, anyone?

COFFEE AND BAKERIES

ALAMO SQUARE CAFE

#coffee #sandwiches #SidewaysLounging

711 Fillmore Street

Sitting on the slope of a residential block, Alamo Square Cafe has all the necessary fuel for your picnic in the painted-lady park. Alamo's a little Mediterranean, with homemade hummus on the menu that you can slap between some bread (with falafel, tomato, cucumber, and tahini) for a light, cheap lunch. The coffee here isn't fancy but does the trick, and if you choose to stay they've got free WiFi and there are tree-shaded outdoor seats on the slanted street.

CANDYBAR

#FancyDessert #wine #cocktails

1335 Fulton Street

This wine, cocktail, and dessert bar has the kind of sweets that finish a white tablecloth meal, but without having to pay for the whole tasting menu. The ice cream sundaes here aren't your typical dairy-drenched bananas; Candybar's version is a fancily arranged

plate of delicate macarons, brûléed bananas, brownies, and, of course, frosty scoops of ice cream serving as the delicious glue. Since Candybar doesn't cater to kids, they can drench their s'mores in booze. It's all a little froufrou, but it's a great place to add a few cavities to your hangover.

CHILE PIES & ICE CREAM

#ChileCheddarApplePie #PieShake #CarbSugarComa

601 Baker Street

You know you've stopped giving a fuck about your thunder thighs when the idea of mixing pie and a milkshake sounds like an excellent snack. For those moments, Chile Pies & Ice Cream has got your fat back. You choose your pie slice and milkshake flavor and these kind people shove the two into each other until you're drinking more calories than you've eaten all week. Aside from liquid heart attacks, these guys have an incredible apple pie that's spiced with green chiles and cheddar and served à la mode (with Three Twins ice cream). They have salads and soups, too, but who the hell cares when there's pie to be had?

MATCHING HALF CAFE

#SightglassCoffee #CoolDécor #neighborhoody

1799 McAllister Street

Matching Half is a cozy corner spot with a wall of windows, a handful of wooden tables, and a comfy reading bench outside. Since it's situated on a mostly residential block, people come here to hang with their dogs and chat over coffee. The décor is simple with some artsy touches, like an indoor planter box wall arrangement; woodshop lightbulb string art in the bathroom; a blue stained-glass window in the top corner; and clean, patterned prints on the walls. They serve Sightglass coffee and limited pastries like muffins, croissants, Bundt cakes, and cookies in little sleeves.

MOJO BICYCLE CAFE
#RitualCoffee #BikeShop
639 Divisadero Street

A sunken café with tree- and cactus-lined outdoor seating and more plants hanging out inside wooly pockets on its walls. They serve Ritual coffee, select pastries, and (really good) sandwiches, with Big Daddy and Lightning Pils on tap. The indoor seating consists of elongated wood tables and metal stools, with one perfect round table at the usually open window. The back of this place is a full-service bike shop, which means you'll see people coming in with their bent handlebars and flat front tires.

THE MILL
#FourBarrelCoffee #JoseyBakerBread #PriceGouging
736 Divisadero Street

The Mill is a collabo between one of the best coffee roasters in San Francisco (Four Barrel) and the city's premier baker (Josey Baker Bread). Given the fame of both, you'd think this place would be loved by all. But then they went and charged $4 for burnt toast and things went to shit. To many, the Mill became a symbol of everything that's wrong with the rising cost of living in this fancy town. So is it an awful place, full of horrible badness? It's actually pretty nice, with tiled white walls, jars of jam, a rack of freshly baked bread, unique pastries, and strong coffee. While The Mill may now be synonymous with price gouging, as long as you stay away from the controversial toast you're in for some good eats.

VINYL COFFEE & WINE BAR
#BlueBottleCoffee #BeerAndWine #PopUpFood
359 Divisadero Street

Vinyl is a large, dark space where the glare of little laptop Apple symbols form constellations around the shop. Once your night vision kicks in, you'll dig the awesome driftwood branch sculpture, dim sconces, and sassy cerulean and orange color combo of the place. They serve Blue Bottle coffee and have a broad selection of beer and wine. Vinyl also hosts food pop-ups on most nights, where you can sample Sneaky's BBQ (Tuesdays and Wednesdays) and Pizza Hacker pizza (Thursdays and Fridays). They fill the void of Saturday through Monday nights with their own menu of meats, cheeses, and delicious composed salads.

EAT

4505 BURGERS & BBQ
#brisket #ParkingLot
705 Divisadero Street

Everyone knows that meat is better eaten outside and 4505 Burgers has just the converted parking lot to prove it. Their spacious lot is decked out with wooden picnic tables and speakers that blast whatever game might be playing. We always judge the quality of a BBQ joint by the juiciness of their brisket, and 4505 passes with dripping colors. They slow-roast their brisket in a wood-fired oven and offer it up on a platter with two sides, tangy house pickles, and a roll for $12. This platter is just the starting point and you can add up to three meats to your plate for $20. The portions aren't huge, but if this little piggy wants to go to town, you can order any of their smoked meats by the pound and throw portion control out the window.

LA URBANA
#CoolDécor #UpScaleMexican
#TreatYourself
661 Divisadero Street

There is no doubt that you can get authentic Mexican in the Mission for a fraction of the price you pay here, but this is newfangled Mexican that showcases the fine-dining scene of Mexico City with special chef-y techniques, like 63-degree eggs and light-handed, refined plating of normally monstrous dishes like quesadillas. Urbana's wide selection of smoky mezcales, and the cocktails crafted from them, are far from sloppy margaritas. The portions are small, the prices are high, the place is packed during brunch, and the décor is hoity (but beautiful).

OTP Tip: If you're still turning your nose up at upscale Mexican, you can hang in La Urbana's garage, which features beer, wine, a black-and-white wraparound mural, and a chill cart port vibe.

LITTLE STAR PIZZA
#DeepDish #FamousFood
846 Divisadero Street

Our New York hearts have a hard time calling deep-dish, casserole-like pies "pizza," but we'd be fools if we didn't recommend Little Star. Now, this pizza isn't a ninety seconds in the 5,000-degree oven type thing. This is Chicago-style pie and will take at least half an hour after you order. Once the pie arrives, you'll begin to understand the craftsmanship behind the $25, twelve-inch pie. The crust isn't doughy or chewy, but rather a perfect cornmeal cradle to the thick layer of sauce, veggies, and cheese, precut into six thick pie slices that you'll finish on your own despite your better judgment.

STATE BIRD PROVISIONS
#AmericanDimSum #FamousFood
1529 Fillmore Street

State Bird is a Michelin-star restaurant and notoriously hard to get into. You have two options: Buy tickets through their automated system one month in advance (released at midnight every day) or wait up to two hours, starting at 5:30 p.m., outside their unmarked door. This might seem like some fussy bullshit, but in this case the crowds are indeed a sign of greatness. State Bird is the epitome of California cuisine with some well-integrated international touches, plus they have a gimmick nobody outside of Chinatown dares to execute. They serve many dishes dim sum–style, where servers wheel around juicy, salty pork belly ($12), among many other small dishes. If playing fine-dining craps isn't your thing, you can order from the "Commendables" section of the menu. Here, you'll find traditionally served, larger dishes that include their namesake CA State Bird with Provisions, which is a crispy quail over onion confit ($18). You can also opt for State Bird's prix fixe menu, a reasonable $75 for a filling meal made up of about twelve small dishes, including dessert.

TOMMY'S JOYNT
#stew #turkey
1101 Geary Boulevard

You'll know that Tommy's isn't trying to be NOPA-fancy the minute you spot the brightly colored, old-school signage from across the street, which welcomes strangers to eat where "Turkey is King!" It's the kind of place where you know things will be greasy, meaty, and cheap. The day crowd at Tommy's is mostly tourists and old people looking for turkey dinners (which they get for under $7, gravy and all). Take advantage of it being open until 2 a.m. daily, stumble up to the counter, and get yourself some hearty buffalo stew, seriously sloppy joes, or spaghetti and meatballs. The portions could knock over a herd of cattle and the prices seem to have carried over from 1947, wh Tommy's first opened.

 SEE AND DO

ALAMO SQUARE
#FullHouse #PaintedLadies
Steiner Street and Hayes Street

At the intersection of Hayes and Steiner, and best viewed from the little hill in Alamo Square Park, you will find "the painted ladies," a row of sloped pastel-colored houses made famous by the *Full House* opening credits. If you don't recognize them right away, you'll hear tourists explain the grand importance of these buildings to their clueless friends. Even though one of the ladies was wearing her scaffolding stockings when we were here, the buildings do bring you back to childhood memories of Uncle Joey's bad jokes and Uncle Jesse's voluminous hair. Aside from the ladies, the park is filled with people walking their dogs, doing yoga, tennis, and picnicking under the tall

FUN FACT

Due to a huge community uprising, tour buses are now banned from driving past and hollering at the ladies.

SF JAZZ FESTIVAL
#free #jazz #food
Fillmore Street between Eddy and Jackson

Every Fourth of July weekend, twelve blocks of Fillmore Street fill with free jazz and fried food. Hopping from stage to stage in this historic district will get you up close to amazing music that ranges from old-man smooth jams to more upbeat, danceable jazz. The food is carney fare, like funnel cakes and dogs, with a bit of a Creole twist. Keeping Fillmore's jazz alive since 1985, this fest brings a lot of soul to the streets every year.

🏪 SHOP

THE PERISH TRUST
#VintageKnickknacks
#FancyArtisanalJunk
728 Divisadero Street

The Perish Trust is decked out with the kind of artisanal goods and products San Francisco is proud to produce. Here, you'll find cards, books, expensive menswear, Western things, belts, backpacks, elixirs, beard-grooming products, and jewelry. Your browsing experience is soundtracked by old-timey guitar sounds and, while expensive, every item is distinctive and has that century-old feel. While a vintage typewriter might be hard to pack in your carry-on, a few leather-bound notebooks printed with local art will fit just fine.

😎 PARTYING

BAR CRUDO
#TreatYourself #HappyHourDeal
655 Divisadero Street

Scrape the dirt from under your nails, then head to Crudo for raw fish. Decorated in clean and dark wood with a steel-lined bar, Crudo creates the perfect cold atmosphere for consuming fresh fish. It looks fancy, but prices aren't terrible, especially if you hit their happy hour (a short 5 to 6:30 p.m.). You'll have to grease up your elbows and squeeze into that bar early, but for your efforts you'll be lavishly rewarded with $1 oysters, slightly spicy jalapeño mussels (also $1), and $6 seafood-loaded chowder.

BARREL HEAD BREWHOUSE
#FunFood #ThreeBuckBeerSpecials
1785 Fulton Street

This brew house is a feel-good operation. Whether you're here for food, booze, or a nighttime schmooze, these guys get it right from all sides. Their food is just greasy enough and coats your gut while being easy on the taste buds. Dishes like TV-dinner favorite Salisbury steak are all dressed up with French onion soup flavors, and their brunch-time poutine (Canadians, listen up) is covered in bits of rendered bacon. As for drinks, there are at least three beers on tap that are made in-house and you can get a flight ($8) to sample all three. All this should be enough to set them apart from the competition, but they take it a step further by allowing you to make your own Manhattan from four components of listed ingredients.

MADRONE ART BAR
#MotownMondays #EclecticSpace
500 Divisadero Street

The first thing you see on the approach is a quirky art display window, like those shoe box dioramas you loved making in first grade. There's also a photo booth right at the entrance to get you at your best. Madrone embraces all kinds of art, from visual to film to music. At any given time, you'll find cool designs all over its walls and sassy, mismatched couches. Madrone hosts exhibits, art parties, themed nights, and film screenings. On Mondays, the bar presents a

The Fillmore

Motown throwback dance party and people come out to get down from all over the city.

MINI BAR SF

#NotYourHotelRoom #cocktails #art
837 Divisadero Street

Right across from Little Star Pizza, come to Mini Bar to take in some local art and grab a predinner cocktail without the fancy mixology prices and snotty service. Aside from the tiny beer bottles along the bar, Mini Bar is just a regular-sized good time, with a makeout space in the back and bouncy black booths.

THE FILLMORE

#legendary #LiveMusic
1805 Geary Boulevard

Ever heard of Jimi Hendrix? How about Prince? The Fillmore has been a favorite venue of bigger-than-big artists (like the Grateful Dead, the Cure, Radiohead, and shit tons more) over the many years of its existence. It started as a dance hall more than a century ago and has changed hands many times since, but always persevered in its mission to bring the art of music to the ears of its loyal patrons. Stepping into the Fillmore will hit you in the face with history. The walls are covered in photos of past performers and the air is thick with star-making potential. It'll hurt your heart that you were born too late to see Jimi get nasty on his guitar here, but if it's any consolation, new legends pass through on the regular.

THE INDEPENDENT

#venue #RangeOfGenres
628 Divisadero Street

The Independent actively tries to stay on top of the game in a wide variety of genres. This place books acts like Ghostface Killah and STRFKR, along with lesser-known artists. The venue itself is small and people rhythmically rub up on each other to the beats. Tickets range from $15 to $35 with special events (like New Year's Eve) at a still reasonable $65. Despite the real estate–driven decline of legit music venues in the city, the Independent is still (cross your fingers) standing strong.

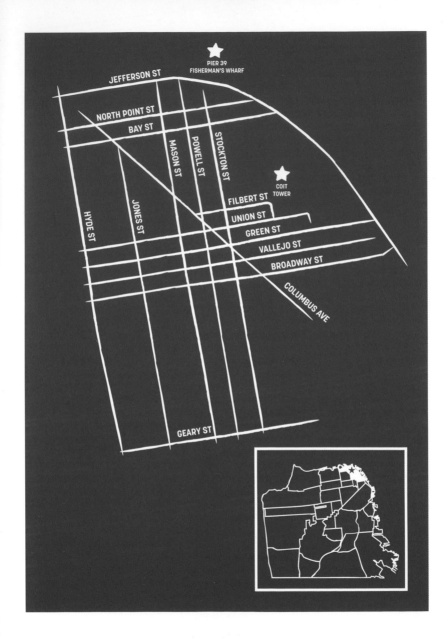

NORTH BEACH/
FISHERMAN'S WHARF

During its Gold Rush heyday as the "Barbary Coast," this area was better known for its criminals, drunks, and a thriving red-light district. When the gold was gone and the 1906 quake struck hard, the area was rebuilt as a port. In the 1950s, Jack Kerouac and his beatniks took up residence at City Lights Bookstore and nearby cafés and bars. While there is a little flavor left from every era (hint: random strippers standing around twiddling their thumbs), this part of the city is best known for being a tourist trap. That doesn't mean you shouldn't break some bread at Boudin, check out everything at Fisherman's Wharf, gorge on Italian in North Beach, or indulge in a little saloon hooch. There is still vintage charm here; you'll just have to wade through the tourists to find it.

COFFEE AND BAKERIES

BEACON COFFEE & PANTRY
#SightglassCoffee #ArtisanalGoods
805 Columbus Avenue

Beacon is a little pricey, but a good find for the neighborhood. They've got plant arrangements on the wall and they serve delicious Sightglass coffee and light breakfast, along with lunch and pastries. What sets them apart is the little grocery store in the back that sells local artisanal goods. The WiFi is strong, there are outlets aplenty, and the baristas are nice enough.

BLACK POINT CAFE
#coffee #lunch #view
882 North Point Street

Black Point naturally attracts tourists because of its proximity to Ghirardelli Square, but it's a good spot for lunch, with tons of seating spread out among three levels with a tree in the middle. Their turkey sandwich is that classic kind with towers of turkey, sprouts, lettuce, and tomato. The baristas are sleepy and Black Point's walls of windows make for gorgeous views. Fight for the bottom-level corner table for the best vantage point.

BUENA VISTA CAFE
#history #IrishCoffee
2765 Hyde Street

Situated right on the path of the Powell-Hyde Street cable car, Buena Vista draws many for brunch; others come for history. We found ourselves at Buena Vista Cafe because they serve boozed-up Irish coffee (plus, you can take it to go!). It started in the '50s when the owner wanted to re-create a drink

he had at an Irish airport. After a lot of fuss trying to find the perfect whiskey and cream combo, their Irish coffee was born and they still follow that same perfect recipe today, serving it up in glasses with floating cream on top. There's no better way to deal with swarms of tourists and their obnoxious children than having a little hooch under your belt before noon.

CAFFE TRIESTE
#OldSchoolEspresso #LiveMusic
609 Vallejo Street

Opened in 1956 by "Papa Gianni" Giotta, Trieste was the first espresso bar on the West Coast. Before laptops and hipster brews, Trieste was the kind of place where creative people, like Jack Kerouac, went to put pen to paper (most of *The Godfather* was written here), down serious amounts of espresso, and listen to live music. Aside from offering WiFi and attracting tourists, this place hasn't changed much over the years; you can still come here to discuss life with an old man over an old-school latte.

GHIRARDELLI

#OGLocation #chocolate #sundaes

900 North Point

While you can buy bags of Ghirardelli Square chocolates at the airport, there's something special about visiting the place where it all started, plus they've got ice cream, hot chocolate, and cookies here. Originally opened in the mid-1800s to service Gold Rush miners looking for a treat, this OG shop is now most famous for their ridiculous sundaes, packed with ice cream, fudge, cookies, and those famous squares of chocolate. This is not a one-man job; bring reinforcements.

HOLE IN THE WALL COFFEE

#JustCoffee

524 Union Street

This place is just a dude in a literal hole with two menu panels behind him and one table with two barstools on the sidewalk. It's like emergency coffee when you realize you're about to hike the Coit Tower and need more fuel. The coffee is Reveal and they offer a blond or brunette roast and a North Beach blend.

LIGURIA BAKERY

#focaccia #HistoricBakery

1700 Stockton Street

You want a muffin, cake, or newfangled pop tart? This is not the place. Family-owned since 1911, Liguria does focaccia and it's the best pizzalike bread you'll ever have. They bake it fresh daily and close the doors once they're all focaccia-ed out. This is the type of bread that grips your nostrils and makes you double-time your spit swallowing. Perfectly crusty, not greasy, and with a bouncy bite, their breads are mostly savory, but sweet varieties are often available, too. Come here early to compete with the out-of-towners who drive for miles to feed their focaccia cravings.

VICTORIA PASTRY COMPANY

#PrincessCake #cannoli

700 Filbert Street

Victoria is all about classic Italian pastries done right. It's a clean shop, where the inside air smells like that sugary, buttery dough you have to resist eating before you bake it. The cannoli are huge and filled with creamy ricotta, and if you're in the mood for cake, their Princess Cake is fantastic. Everyone behind the counter is eager to feed you, as if they're your long-lost Italian grandmothers.

XOX TRUFFLES

#FreeCandy #BoozeTruffles

754 Columbus Avenue

XOX takes the crack dealer approach to selling you truffles. With every coffee you purchase, the eager Frenchman, owner Jean-Marc Gorce, will throw in a free truffle. But then you'll eat it and fall into a deep debate with yourself about whether you can justify just one more. With flavors like cognac, honey vodka, tequila cayenne, and caffeinated French roast, there's no way you can have just one. That's how the truffle crumbles, friends.

 # EAT

BOUDIN SOURDOUGH BAKERY & CAFE

#HistoricSourdough #chowder

251 Geary Street

This is not just a bakery, but a full-on sourdough complex with a bistro, store, and museum. Boudin has been nursing its sourdough starter since 1849, and it has become one of the most recognizable tastes of San Francisco. The touristy thing to do is to get a sourdough bread bowl filled with their equally famous clam chowder ($14.95) from their bistro, tour the museum, and read up on their bready history. Once all the bread you consumed has settled, head to their store to stock up on a few loaves to maniacally rip chunks from for the next few days.

CARMEL PIZZA COMPANY

#PizzaTrailer #WoodBurningOven

2826 Jones Street

Carmel is an outdoor pizza trailer with good, simple pizza and expansive, plant-covered, heated patio seating. Every pie is made in their old, straight-from-Florence, wood-burning oven that gives the top that bubbly char. Pizzas are $11–$17, and the Quattro Formaggi is a pungent combo of melted cheeses. Each pie is served on a little red-checkered piece of paper for extra Italian flair.

DON PISTO'S

#SitdownMex #BottomlessMimosas

510 Union Street

This isn't trying to be Mission Mexican; Don Pisto's is a huge space with dark wood planks running high up the walls and windows that

funnel in sexy rays of light. The menu is Mex-Remix, which will piss off anybody looking for greasy meat and burrito logs. It's a fork-and-knife date place for when you're still craving a little Mexican, but don't want black beans and sauce running down your arm. They've got Mexican sashimi, fancy sit-down tacos, and pork chops.

È TUTTO QUA
#Italian #pasta
510 Union Street

North Beach is packed with Italian restaurants and picking one becomes a daunting task when you're hungry. È Tutto is a solid choice, with all the pasta you'd ever want and at a price that's not inflated for tourists. All their pastas are made in-house daily, and the cannoli are filled to order. They're known for their all-black squid ink pasta ($17.95) overflowing with mussels, clams, and shrimp. The space is large, the crowd skews older, and truffles make several appearances on the menu if that's your thing.

GOLDEN BOY PIZZA
#GarlicClamPizza #SquareSlices
542 Green Street

Golden Boy's neon pointing-hand sign attracts hungry drunks like a glowing flytrap. Once you've seen the light, you'll be faced with a sheet of square options. At Golden Boy, they only do Sicilian-type slices, where toppings are baked onto focaccia and then cut into squares. If you're not too drunk for shellfish, try out the garlic clam slice ($3.75), a briny, flavorful pizza with a big handful of clams scattered about.

IN-N-OUT BURGER
#CABurgerLegend #AnimalStyle
333 Jefferson Street

If you're not from California and you don't know about this spot, you must try it right here, right now. It's a huge chain, but these are legendary burgers that you can't get anywhere outside of Cali. Here's the plan: Go in there like a pro and order a double cheeseburger—animal style—with both kinds of onions, and if you're feeling brave, get a

side of animal-style fries. These things aren't gourmet in any way, but they are mighty tasty. Once you've had one, you'll be in a cultish secret club of people who have seen the way. Ignore the weird Bible quotes on the bottom of their drink cups.

FUN FACT

We have friends who have moved away from California and had their family ship In-N-Out burgers to them across the country. Seriously.

MARIO'S BOHEMIAN CIGAR STORE CAFE
#MeatballSub #espresso
566 Columbus Avenue

This place is filled with drunks in the middle of the day with sauce all over their happy faces. It's an old-school Italian joint with a feel-good vibe. The right way to do Mario's is to go here for lunch, order a beer and a meatball sub, then finish it off with an espresso to perk you back to normal. Mario's makes their subs on Liguria's famous focaccia, lightly toasted, perfectly sauced, and stuffed with meaty goodness. While a cigar would be a good finisher, they stopped selling them after CA banned smoking inside.

MOLINARI DELICATESSEN
#sandwiches #HangingMeat
566 Columbus Avenue

Stepping through the doors of Molinari means entering a palace of hanging salami, smelly cheese wheels, and old-world charm. Molinari is like the inside of an Italian wine cask, and the long counter, with all their

fridge offerings on display, will draw you to it like a magnetic field of sandwich possibilities. Take a number, pick any sandwich, watch the guys scurry to make it, and kick out whoever is sitting at the two tables on the sidewalk.

SAM'S
#burgers #DrunkFood #HoleInTheWall
504 Broadway Street

Sam won't take any of your bullshit at 3 a.m. What he will do, though, is serve you the kind of greasy, messy, shitty cheeseburger and fries your inner fat kid wants at that hour after a long night of kicking your liver in the teeth. Sam's is kitschy with random signs packed into the tight space and a sizzling grill visible from the foggy window. Bourdain's been here; beware of his groupies.

SOTTO MARE
#FreshSeafood #cioppino #FamousFood
552 Green Street

Let the swordfish hanging up front lead the way to one of the most famous seafood stews in the country. You will have to wade through a sea of granddads to get to a table, but trust us, this isn't old-people food. The cioppino at Sotto Mare is an edible landmark, and while it costs $41 (enough for two), it's stuffed with fresh seafood and the broth is so flavorful you'll drool all over yourself (for which they have bibs). Aside from amazing food, the restaurant has the perfect amount of kitsch, Italian family togetherness, and a hint of gangster in the air.

THE CODMOTHER FISH AND CHIPS
#FishAndChips #trailer
2824 Jones Street

If you've ever been in a fish and chips argument with a Brit, get ready to add some fuel to the fire. Whatever they have across the pond does not compare to Codmother. Take that to the bank. In a tiny trailer with some chairs outside, they fry up their fish super crispy and, for only $9.95, you get two huge pieces, plus "chips" (or fries—as we say in proper English). Squeeze a little vinegar on, dip them into baja sauce, and let that flaky fish win your heart.

FUN FACT
This place is owned and operated by Suzanne Acevedo, a really friendly British lady. We're just talking all that Brit shit for a little fun.

TANGUITOS
#BigAssBurgers #cheap
2850 Jones Street

Tanguitos is a little, unassuming truck with the words ARGENTINEAN EMPANADAS AND BURGERS written up top. First of all, when have you ever had an Argentinean burger? It makes perfect sense; the nation eats more meat than anybody else on the planet, but we've never pegged them for burger types. We were all wrong. The burgers you get here are like smashing every meat found on a parrilla (which they have) between buns and calling it lunch. It's a three-fister, ten-napkin event, and will only run you $7.

TONY'S PIZZA NAPOLETANA
#AllStyles #FamousFood
2850 Jones Street

To quiet all the thin crusters, deep-dishers, and Sicilian scoundrels, this joint makes pizza in every style imaginable. Run by Tony Gemignani, an eleven-time pizza world champion (because there is such a thing!), Tony's is where he shows off his ability to make whatoverthefuck kind of pizza you like (using different ovens to achieve distinct styles). We're not going to pick favorites, but a pizza place with Tony in its name can never be that bad.

VIETNAM RESTAURANT
#tiny #BestBánhMì
620 Broadway Street

A tiny hole in an unexpected place, this restaurant makes a ridiculis bánh mì. The pork is sautéed and flavorful, the pickled veggies are tangy and crunchy, and the French bread is the right texture. Served with heaps of cilantro, these sandwiches are perfectly crafted by two old ladies who have been doing this for years.

◉ | SEE AND DO

ALCATRAZ
#landmark #prison

The Hornblower (a hybrid eco ferry) departs from Pier 33 several times a day to everyone's favorite high-security prison. Alcatraz floats peacefully in the bay, just waiting for you to explore its inescapable charms. Here, you'll see the living quarters of our country's biggest criminals, explore its lush gardens, and

learn about the island's history (prison and beyond). Most families tour the island during the day, but the best time to visit is at night. Prices hover around $30–$40, and you should reserve your tour online. They often hold interesting art exhibits on Alcatraz Island, and if you've got a few more hours to spare, you can hop over to Angel Island (the Ellis Island of the West) for a combo tour.

COIT TOWER
#views #CoolHistory
1 Telegraph Hill Boulevard

The Coit Tower looks like a relic lookout left behind by the military but was actually funded by wealthy Lillie Coit in an effort to beautify her favorite part of town. To see her pretty tower, hike up the Union Street

sidewalk stairs (or take Filbert Steps for a more scenic route up). The inside of the tower features a 360-degree painted mural of the industrial history of California. A little gift shop is tucked into its coils, and you can take the elevator to the top observation deck for a full view of the city for $8. Alternatively, you can opt for the views from Pioneer Park, which surrounds the tower at the base.

FILBERT STEPS
#WalkThroughGardens
#WorkYourQuads
Filbert Street and Sansome Street

A winding stairway that will take you through hillside houses with gorgeous gardens and pathways covered in California wildflowers. We don't care who you are, this walk will turn you into a fairy princess. Angel's trumpets hang low and it's a long way up (or down), but so nice. Follow the sign directly in front of Levi Plaza on Sansome and Filbert to the unmarked stairs hugging the hillside, and let the fairyland adventure unfold.

FUN FACT

Lillie Coit was once a bad-ass woman who often dressed like a dude, drank like a sailor, and gambled with the best of them.

House) but serve famed Dungeness crab that's caught right off the Wharf. This is a fun, build-your-own-adventure type of place that even locals can get behind.

SAN FRANCISCO MARITIME NATIONAL HISTORICAL PARK
#OldShips #CheapFun
499 Jefferson Street

At the terminal stop of the Powell-Hyde cable car sits a fleet of floating ships that you can explore for only $5. The Balclutha—a massive sailing ship built in 1886—is the star of this show, and you can access her many rooms and parlors, restored to their shabby chic glory. There are also two tugboats, three schooners, a steam ferryboat, and a land-sitting houseboat, each with bits of maritime history inside.

FISHERMAN'S WHARF
#TouristMecca #seals #museums #seafood

As much as locals try to avoid this place at all costs, they love it just the same. At one time, the Wharf was entirely industrious, and while a good amount of fishery still happens here, the city poured millions into renovating the area to create San Francisco's biggest outdoor tourist attraction. You can spend a full day here, doing a number of things. Our favorites include the Magowan's Infinite Hall of Mirrors ($5), a mirror maze that'll make you a little nauseous; watching the seals hang out on the docks at Pier 39 (free); Musée Mécanique, a video and arcade museum with games from all eras (bring a bag of quarters); and the Musical Stairs, created by the same guy who got Tom Hanks to hop in *Big*. The Wharf is packed with seafood restaurants, and most are expensive and über touristy (like Forbes Island and Crab

FUN FACT

The Farallon Islands are twenty-seven miles off the coast and are a feeding area for great whites.

TATTOO CITY
#EdHardy #TurnYourShirtsToTats
700 Lombard Street

Ed Hardy started putting his art to skin in the Mission in 1977, and this shop is the third incarnation of the original parlor. He put skin art on fabric to build an empire of tatted tees shortly thereafter. We may not love the douche bags who wear his stuff, but the man is no doubt an innovator and a tattoo legend. His shop is a big space and the artists here have varied styles. While Ed is now retired, his son Doug is around to turn that fake tat long-sleeved shirt into the real thing.

SHOP

101 MUSIC
#FunkyJunk #OldRecords
513 Green Street

A tiny shop super stuffed with random musical shit, 101 is the kind of place that gentrification can't touch. To effectively browse this place, you'll have to take short, side-to-side steps. There's a Lonely Hearts poster on the door, guitars hanging from the ceiling, old speakers, stacks of sheet music, and a basement filled with random crates of records.

CITY LIGHTS BOOKSTORE
#BeatGeneration #HistoricBookstore
261 Columbus Avenue

A literary landmark, this longstanding indie bookstore and publisher began during the beat generation (est. 1953) with the goal of focusing on progressive and anti-authoritarian publications. Many a beatnik has traveled through here to read the texts between its walls, and you can come enjoy three floors of anarchic-centric books. They carry a large selection of literature (new and old), collectible editions and sets, and their own published texts. The wall art is inspiring and political, the staff leaves you alone to browse, and there's a whole room dedicated to poetry upstairs with a chair and a thinking window with a view.

PARTYING

GINO & CARLO COCKTAIL LOUNGE
#ItalianDive #BYOPizza
548 Green Street

This is a divey place where you go to get in touch with your inner good-for-nothing Italian. Gino's is a no-nonsense neighborhood bar that gathers a lot of local characters. There's a ratty pool table, $4 stiff cocktails, and they let you bring in pizza from Golden Boy next door.

MAGGIE MCGARRY'S
#Irish #DanceParties
1560 Powell Street

While this bar only opened in 2006, it sits on historic music ground. Their stage has seen the likes of Janis Joplin and the Doors, among many others who performed before little, wee Maggie was born. Now this same stage welcomes mostly cover bands that make for

fun weekend dance parties. Some of the bartenders are actually Irish, and not only can they talk pretty, but they'll also mix you up a drink of Irish strength and only charge you chump change (average $5 for well).

NORTHSTAR CAFE
#sports #BarCrawls
1560 Powell Street

Northstar is by no means a café; rather, it's a sports-centric bar that's been around since 1882. Things get wild here during game days, but not as douchey as other places we've been. They hook you up with free baskets of popcorn, beers are $3 during happy hour (until 7-ish), and there's a free pool table. Hordes of college kids will sometimes roll through here on bar crawls, and Sunday nights are always all about football.

SPECS' TWELVE ADLER MUSEUM CAFE
#CoolJunkDécor #OldManStories
12 Williams Place

This bar has a special place in our hearts. Off an alley and up a little hill, Specs' is a hidden spot, the inside of which looks like you've crawled into an old man's memory box. The walls are covered in weird shit that Spec himself has collected over his colorful lifetime. Is that a walrus penis bone over the bar? As a matter of fact it is. Spec is usually lingering around in a leather jacket, hitting on everything with a heartbeat, telling absurd stories about Eskimos and the way North Beach used to be. You will stumble out of here a changed soul, no longer afraid of getting old.

THE SALOON
#OldestBarInSF #music
1232 Grant Avenue

The oldest bar in San Francisco, the Saloon has seen its share of wild times since it opened in 1861. The space is a faded wood box that's mostly decorated by the sounds of live jazz Thursday through Sunday (with

rockabilly Mondays). There's a one-drink minimum, but shows are otherwise free and drinks run between $4 and $6. While tourists pop in for the historic value and disperse once the music starts, the dancing crowd is normally a clusterfuck of happy, local drinkers with good intentions.

VESUVIO
#CoolDécor #BeatHistory
255 Columbus Avenue

If you want to get a taste of the Beat Generation, Vesuvio, perhaps the most famous bar in these parts, is on the path toward drunken enlightenment. Across from City Lights Bookstore, Vesuvio's mosaic décor, eclectic art, and lofted seating has inspired progressive conversation since 1948. Beat poets, including Jack Kerouac, called this their local hangout, and now swarms of tourists (and locals alike) make it theirs.

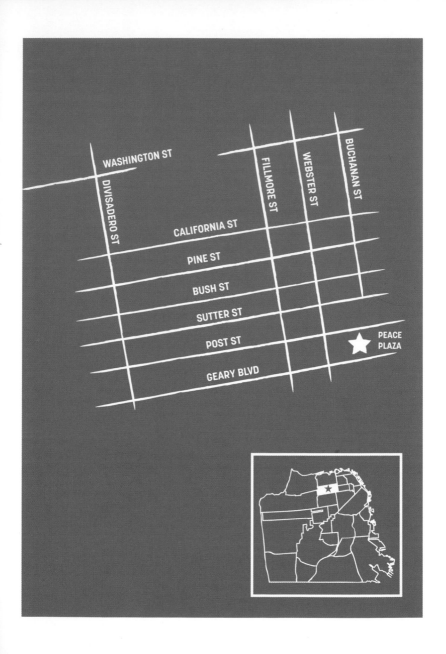

PACIFIC HEIGHTS/ JAPANTOWN

Pacific Heights is home to expensive brand-name stores and the people who can afford them. One thing we know about rich people is that they're into some weird shit, and Pacific Heights reinforces that notion. Come here to window-shop, treat yourself to a hunk of millionaire's bacon at Sweet Maple or a dildo brunch at Red Door Cafe, check out Danielle Steele's ugly mansion, then let go at Audium, where music is sculpted in the dark. Nearby Japantown is a pocket of distinct culture, where you'll find mochi bakeries, simple sushi, and an entire mall full of Japanese merch.

☕ COFFEE AND BAKERIES

B. PATISSERIE

#dessert #MacaronTree

2821 California Street

Some pastry chefs spend their entire lives trying to perfect the delicate macaron. When you walk into a bakery and they've chosen to use these holy French edibles

as mere wall decorations, you know they're doing some next-level shit over there. Every pastry is masterfully crafted and their flaky, butter Kouign Amman is off-the-charts delicious. Go for a tart, some pudding (with a macaron on top), or anything in the pastry case; you won't be disappointed.

BENKYODO COMPANY

#historic #mochi

1747 Buchanan Street

Most Americans only recently warmed up to mochi, but Benkyodo is one of the first businesses in Japantown and has been hand-making mochi for over one hundred years. Supple and with that perfect doughy, flour-dusted shell, the mochi at Benkyodo are

YakiniQ

available in a huge variety of flavors (in addition to the classics) and are only about $1.25 apiece. They sell out fast, especially the blueberry mochi, so get there early and buy a dozen.

JANE (ON FILLMORE)

#StumptownCoffee #lunch
2123 Fillmore Street

Two levels of super-chic black décor with clashy patterns all around, Jane is a fancy spot for coffee or a $10–$12 lunch. Owned by pastry chef Amanda Michael, Jane is named after her daughter and filled with chef-y baked goods. Go for a well-prepared classic blueberry muffin and keep an eye out for gooey sticky buns on the weekends. They serve Stumptown coffee and have laptop-free tables to keep things moving.

THE SOCIAL STUDY

#café #bar #BangingBathroom
1795 Geary Boulevard

You'd be screwed out of luck if you came here to study. Among the many distractions, there are really good-looking guys day-drinking at the bar, the bartender/barista is really nice (and pretty hot), and the music taps into an upbeat vein of old-school hip-hop, like Method Man and old Dre. The books lining the perimeter are just for show; the real business here is in the bathroom, where you'll find an all-black toilet, Prince poster, slanted full-length mirror, a disco ball, and a sturdy lock, which to us means that studying is the last thing they want you to do in this place.

YAKINIQ CAFE

#SweetPotatoLatte #macaroons
1640 Post Street

Of all things, a sweet potato seems like the last thing anybody would ever put in (or even next to) a latte. At YakiniQ, they purée sweet potato, froth it up with milk, serve it to you in a cup, and you know what? It's fucking delicious. This spot is strange and the service is spotty, but they throw some unexpected, Japanese-inspired flavors together that seem to work every time.

EAT

ELLA'S
#brunch #American #StickyBuns
500 Presidio Avenue

For those mornings when you wake up wanting something hearty and all-American, Ella's is cooking up an egg-and-bacon storm with little fancy twists. They throw roasted chicken onto their hash and bake their own biscuits fresh daily. Their omelets are always perfectly cooked and with seasonal ingredients, the pancakes are fluffy, and if all you want is a warm pastry for breakfast, the sticky buns ($5.75) are top-loaded with pecans and pull apart gloriously.

LA BOULANGE ON PINE
#bakery #bread #AfterHoursDinner
2325 Pine Street

In addition to the same high-quality baked goods available at other locations of this SF über chain, La Boulange on Pine offers something special. On weekends, they host a first-come-first-served $20 prix fixe, after-hours dinner. The exact menu changes based on what they feel like making, but they often have roasted chicken, several sides, and, of course, dessert. They don't serve booze, but you can bring your own and there's no corking fee.

RED DOOR CAFE
#DildoBrunch #TreatYourself
1608 Bush Street

The food equivalent of morning sex, Red Door not only serves a quirky, delicious brunch, but will also hit you in the face with dildos bright and early. Everything on the menu is flamboyant, like the No One Sucks It Like a Straight Man from Texas, and presented as ridiculously as it's described. They don't serve booze, but you can play ring around the penis on your table while you wait.

ROAM ARTISAN BURGERS
#burgers #GourmetFries
1923 Fillmore Street

Roam serves fancy burgers on fancy buns with fancy fries in a fancy place with a backlit bar. The burgers are huge and made with a variety of meats, like heritage bison, then served on huge buns that hold up all those juices. Don't leave here without trying all their fries, which you can accomplish with the fry-fecta ($5.99), or three heaping portions of their sweet potato, regular russet, and haystack fries.

SWEET MAPLE
#brunch #BottomlessWeekdays
2101 Sutter Street

A brunch spot with a cult following, Sweet Maple is best known for its deep-fried

French toast and millionaire's bacon, or two hunks of maple syrup-soaked bacon ($7). This place gets so packed that even those without claustrophobia may have a panic attack. Get a soju Bloody Mary or the $17 bottomless mimosas to calm your nerves. It may be a bit of a circus, but the food is so good they deserve all the hype.

TATAKI SUSHI AND SAKE BAR

#sushi #FlamingTuna
2815 California Street

Tataki is a tiny, charming sushi place with Japanese chefs and white boy waiters that's all about sustainable fishing. All rolls are creatively presented, with the Extinguisher Roll—a spicy tuna roll served with flaming salt—being the most extreme. Tataki is a good place to go alone and sit at the bar,

groove to the rhythmic tunes rolling from the speakers, and partake in happy hour (until 7 p.m.) where it's $4 for basic rolls (Cal, veg, sweet potato) and $3 for hand rolls.

WOODHOUSE FISH CO.

#cioppino #LobsterRolls #DollarOysters
1914 Fillmore Street

From their décor to the menu offerings, Woodhouse is all about the fish. That warm, buttery, rich seafood you crave on foggier days is done to perfection here. Great for oysters ($1 on Tuesdays), Maine lobster rolls, creamy chowder, and reasonably priced cioppino ($29) served with delicious garlic bread to sop up whatever your utensils may miss. Their Castro location is just as good and the décor will make you feel like a fine fisherman.

SF's Best Mini-Chains

From pastries to sex toys, these places perfected their craft and expanded their businesses to multiple locations. While we normally stay away from chains, these local mini-chains are too good to avoid.

EL FAROLITO
OG Location: 2950 24th Street

A messy, late-night Mexican food joint that blew up big. Watch workers chop meat and magically roll up their burritos at super speeds from the line here at 1 a.m. Stock up on plenty of salsa and pickled condiments, then walk the streets knowing that you're holding one of the best burritos in the country.

GOOD VIBRATIONS
OG Location: 603 Valencia Street

A sex shop started and run by women, Good Vibrations never feels grimy. The shop carries all the newest gadgets and is a comfortable place to talk about your most repressed fantasies.

LA BOULANGE
OG Location: 2325 Pine Street

The biggest of the mini-chains, and recently bought out by Starbucks, this French-inspired bakery bistro is popping up in just about every neighborhood. Their baked

goods are consistently amazing and the décor at every single one feels like a trip to the countryside.

PATXI'S PIZZA

OG Location: 511 Hayes Street

If you dig Chicago-style deep dish, this is the place for an affordable, delicious pie. Patxi's has nine locations in SF, and each is always packed. Call ahead so your pizza will be ready by the time you get there.

PHILZ

OG Location: 3101 24th Street

Started by a cute old man who fell in love with coffee, this may look like a generic Peet's, but it's far from. Each cup is crafted by hand, and you'll find Phil himself sipping on a mint mojito iced coffee on the bench outside.

SUPER DUPER BURGERS

OG Location: 2304 Market Street

Ignore the lame name; Super Duper has legit burgers made with Niman Ranch beef and a big name restaurateur (Adriano Paganini of Beretta, Starbelly, and Delarosa) behind the menu. Plus, at $5 a patty, these are undoubtedly the cheapest gourmet burgers in the city.

SUSHIRRITO

OG Location: 226 Kearny Street

It's exactly what you think: a burrito but made with sushi ingredients. This is a fast-food joint, but they use sustainable fish and you get a two-fister lunch for less than the price of a California roll.

👁 SEE AND DO

AUDIUM
#SoundsInTheDark #UniqueExperience
1616 Bush Street

Relying on the idea that when you lose one sense the others are amplified, Audium turns off the lights to perk up your ears. Not really a concert or a club, Audium is a sound experience with different noises and tunes flowing through your body via 169 speakers. The audience is seated in concentric circles, and the sloped walls provide maximum amplification and distribution of sounds. This isn't just a push-button situation; a "sound sculptor" manipulates recorded tracks, creating art out of noise. It's $20 to press PLAY.

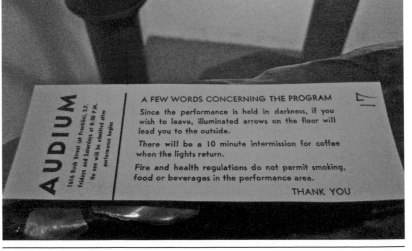

AUDIUM
1616 Bush Street (at Franklin), S.F.
Fridays and Saturdays at 8:30 P.M.
No one will be admitted after performance begins

A FEW WORDS CONCERNING THE PROGRAM

Since the performance is held in darkness, if you wish to leave, illuminated arrows on the floor will lead you to the outside.

There will be a 10 minute intermission for coffee when the lights return.

Fire and health regulations do not permit smoking, food or beverages in the performance area.

THANK YOU

CHERRY BLOSSOM FESTIVAL
#JapaneseStreetFood #TaikoDrums

An annual celebration of SF's Japanese culture, the Cherry Blossom Festival spans two weekends in April. There are parades, traditional Japanese crafts, elaborate flower floats, educational exhibits, and an array of Japanese street food. The coolest thing here is the Taiko drum performance, a loud spectacle traditionally put on to ward off evil spirits with thunderous sounds.

KABUKI SPRINGS & SPA
#ColdPools #HotPools #CucumberEyes
1750 Geary Boulevard

While massages and extra services here get really expensive, the communal part of the spa is only $25. Kabuki is super clean, the staff will treat you like backpacker royalty, and the entry fee grants access to a hot and cold pool, sauna, and steam room where you can get cucumbers laid over your eyes and you can get scrubbed down with salt. It's coed on Tuesdays where you must cover your junk, or you can go on your gender day and let it all hang out.

SPRECKELS MANSION
#DanielleSteele #UglyHedge
2080 Washington Street

Sugar tycoon Adolph Spreckels originally built this limestone mansion, with more rooms than you have toes and fingers, for his trophy wife, Alma de Bretteville. The house is a monstrosity, displaced eight Victorians during its construction, and is made more ridiculous by a giant, wraparound hedge that too-cool-for-school romance writer (and current owner) Danielle Steele put up to keep all the little people out.

SHOP

JAPAN CENTER MALL

#JapaneseKnickknacks #OddlyEmpty
1581 Webster Street

This is a weird, eerily empty mall with two wings (east and west) that surrounds Japantown's Peace Plaza. The plaza often holds various events (we saw real Sumo wrestling here), and the mall wings house a bunch of overstocked Japanese stores, the busiest of which is Daiso Japan, a supermarket and kitsch shop. Take advantage of its lack of crowds and browse the small shops where you can find anything from ridiculous car accessories to Hello Kitty stationery, then treat yourself to some Nitro ice cream at Chocolate Chair.

PARTYING

BOOM BOOM ROOM

#LiveMusic #jazz #HipHop
1601 Fillmore Street

A historic, intimate venue with a lot of soul, Boom Boom Room hosts underground acts in every genre, and the décor—with its checkered floors and blue Christmas lights—has an old-school, raging music-scene vibe. It's a good place to get down to some funk or jazz, and tickets to most events are never over $10. Our favorite night is Return of the Cypher (ROTC), a Sunday-night freestyle hip hop show that throws down hard and costs nada.

LION PUB

#cocktails #décor
2062 Divisadero Street

A good spot for cheap(er) cocktails, the Lion always mixes a strong margarita ($8) and they make greyhounds ($7) by squeezing a real, live grapefruit into a glass. No gross syrups, not ever. It's covered in glass, mirrors, and windows, and feels a lot fancier than it is. Are there lions? As a matter of fact, yes.

SAN FRANCISCO ATHLETIC CLUB

#SportsBar #BeerBathtub
1750 Divisadero Street

As the name suggests, this bar is all about sports, of every kind, all the time. It's fully loaded with everything you want (and sometimes hate) about a sports bar, including a bunch of TVs, screaming fans, and appropriate bar food (wings and burgers, check). Plus, if you're really making a night out of whatever game you're watching, they'll bring a bathtub of beer to your table, it's twenty-four bottles for $80-$100, depending on how expensive your tastes are.

SWANK COCKTAIL & COFFEE CLUB

#NotSwank #fireplace
488 Presidio Avenue

This bar is "swank" in the most ironic of ways. Like the set from a mid-'60s ski bunny porno flick, Swank's got shag, sassy posters, and a fireplace. It's not run-down enough to be a dive, but it's also not classy enough for overthought cocktails. Swank is the premier place to wear your chartreuse sweaters and loafers, lounge by the fire, and engage in a raging round of trivia every Wednesday night.

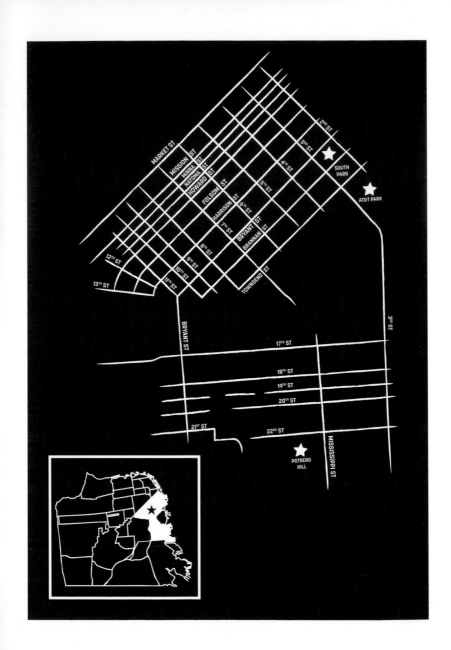

SOMA/
POTRERO HILL/
DOGPATCH

SOMA (South of Market) is like an Escher maze of office buildings with cool spots nestled in the crevices. Here, you'll find fancy cocktails, microbreweries, fancily extracted coffee, and buttoned-up yet stylish professionals. There's an entire trailer park full of food trucks, and in certain parts you'll feel the thriving motorcycle culture. SOMA's also got a kinky side, best seen at the Folsom Street Fair, where leather whips and ass chaps replace briefcases and pants. To the South, Dogpatch carries a bit of the SOMA vibe with a layer of brick and industry. A steep step up, Potrero Hill is full of creative studios, auto-body garages, and incredible bird's-eye views of SOMA down below.

COFFEE AND BAKERIES

CAFFE CENTRO
#yuppie #MiddleOfSouthPark
102 South Park

Centro is in the middle of South Park, and it looks like a Universal Studios set. This café feels like a first-floor corner living room with a window for every foot of wall space. You'll be transported to a small town in the middle of busy SOMA, and every seat in the house is airy and beautiful with houseplants all around. Aside from coffee, they serve light lunch fare and play chill music to match the décor. While Centro is super yuppie, with lots of men laptopping and meeting with other men, the park views are unbeatable.

FARLEY'S
#coffee #mags #PotreroHill
1315 18th Street

Like a classy old chair made new with a fresh coat of paint, Farley's is one part old-timey and two parts über chic. This café feels like a parlor, and some of the baristas have British accents. They serve De La Paz coffee, Starter Bakery pastries, Three Twins ice cream, and empanadas from nearby El Porteño. There's also a little magazine store in the back corner, big built-in booths near the windows, and going to the bathroom means walking up some rickety stairs as if you're climbing into an indoor tree house. Farley's is laptop-friendly (with plenty of outlets) and will often make you feel like whipping out your monocle and getting your shoes shined.

FRONT CAFE
#garage #IcedCoffee
1 Front Street

Behind a roll-up garage door that says NEVER, EVER, EVER, NEVER PARK HERE sits a clean, white-tiled coffee lab with giant glass beakers that cover exquisite pastries and other scientific glassware serving coffee-related purposes. Come here for their iced coffee, which comes in a mason jar with a lid that you get to keep (maybe; we kept ours) and is served with a giant, rectangular ice cube in the middle that melts slowly and evenly. It's expensive ($5.25) and they ask you to "experience" it in its purest form before mucking it up with milk and sugar. At first you'll curse them for being pretentious dicks, and then you'll realize that it really doesn't need anything.

FROZEN KUHSTERD
#BetterThanAnIceCreamTruck
#CrazyFlavors
150 Mississippi Street

Frozen Kuhsterd is denser and silkier than ice cream. These guys peddle the weirdest flavors—like ube, Thai tea, affogato, and cereal milk (that you can top with corn flakes). All were inspired by the world travels of its proprietor. As if their own flavor creations weren't unique enough, this truck partners with local coffee, doughnut, cookie, chocolate, boba, and other confectionery crafters to turn their cream into sandwiches, sundaes, and ridiculous mounds of pure mouth bliss.

MR. AND MRS. MISCELLANEOUS
#IceCream #FuckLunch
699 22nd Street

The larger-than-life, fourteen-scoop ice cream cone painted on the outside banister will lead you into a place of frozen wonder. Forgo lunch so you can stuff yourself with rich and creamy dessert instead. These are adult flavors, but they will put you in a sugar coma just the same. Each scoop is $4, but you'll want to get at least three from the daily rotation (eight to ten flavors at a time). Jasmine green tea, plus anything malted or with brown butter, are at the top of our list.

PINKIE'S BAKERY
#sweet #savory #inventive
1196 Folsom Street

The pastries here look like they came straight out of a coloring book, and their lemon bars, salted doughnuts, and fluffernutters will put you in a sweet chokehold. Pinkie's doesn't do dainty, so while your baked good of choice may be $4 and up, these portions will take a marathon to burn off. On Saturdays, they get crazy on their doughnuts and throw whatever the fuck they want all over the top.

RED DOOR COFFEE
#FourBarrelCoffee #ArtGallery
111 Minna Street

Red Door is a coffee shop in the morning, a lounge at night, and an amazing art gallery all the time. Go for the coffee shop part when they serve Four Barrel coffee and

enjoy the art without the douche crowd that gathers later on (when there's a $10 cover). It's a huge, posh gallery space with incredible art on the walls, museum bench seating, tree trunk rounds for tables, double windows with black velvet curtains, and accents of beautiful wood chunks throughout. They're not kidding about the red door, which is a massive, decked-out, ornate Chinese palace gate, and, if you look closely, a Darth Vader ATM.

SHOWPLACE CAFFE
#CharmingOwner
#ShootingTheShitOverCoffee
715 Brannan Street

The barista/owner, Ryan, is awesome, and don't let Yelp tell you otherwise. His sense of humor is dry, and if you don't get it, it's your own damn fault. He will tell you everything about this city if you ask. We listened in on a conversation between him and a young backpacking couple, where he gave them a slew of recommendations about beer bars

and Vietnamese sandwiches. Get a custardy and purposefully burnt cannele (candlelight) with your coffee, settle into the comfy chairs next to the record player, and enjoy the feeling of hanging out in Ryan's garage.

SIGHTGLASS COFFEE
#CoffeeCult #MassiveLoft
270 7th Street

An industrial barn loft with bike parking on the side, Sightglass is always bustling with special coffee business. Along with mustachioed regulars ordering their brew from busy baristas, employees are constantly "cupping," tasting, mulling about with beans, and doing paperwork upstairs at the third-level balcony. That work pays off, as their espresso is black, glistening, creamy, and not at all bitter. A standing bar wraps around the whole place, there's seating upstairs underneath wooden beamed ceilings, stools overlook the main floor, and a white taxidermied owl watches over the place.

VEGA AT LANGTON
#CoffeeShack #ScooterCentral
1246 Folsom Street

Vega looks makeshift, but someone definitely put thought into this shanty scooter shack. A hole in the wall with only a few seats up front, the raw space inside is full of more scooters than people. The other décor elements include a vintage Isle of Man poster and framed pictures of James Dean doubles (with their scooters). Their coffee concoctions, like the Dirty Macau Iced Coffee (sweetened condensed milk, espresso, and ice) and the Grand Prix Julep (featuring peppermint rose simple syrup!), are just as sly as the décor. There's a lot of flavor in this small space, and all the employees ride in on . . . (you guessed it).

EAT

CITIZEN'S BAND
#American #MacAndCheese #dessert
1198 Folsom Street

Citizen's Band serves comforting favorites that are elevated but not cut down to bird-food portions. Their tower of mac and cheese is an edible sculpture with fat onion rings stacked atop a slab of creamy mac and a liberal drizzle of cheese sauce. It'll put a smile on your face and a stent in your heart. Deviled eggs, a fantastic burger, pork chops, and fried chicken are all on the menu, and since they're owned by the same no-nonsense people as Pinkie's Bakery next door, you know that dessert will be good.

DELI BOARD
#sandwiches #MenuChangesDaily
1058 Folsom Street

A modern deli with a small selection of rotating sandwiches daily; you never know what Deli Board is brewing. No matter when you pop in, we assure you that every one of their creations is absolutely amazing,

stuffed with fresh ingredients in interesting combinations, and they never skimp on meat or sauce. You'll have to relinquish control, put your hunger in their hands, and trust that they'll take care of you.

OTP Tip: Their sister restaurant, Rye Project, is a "newish" sort of Jewish deli with a punk vibe and a set menu. The Kapash—a half corned beef and half pastrami on rye—will blow you away.

DEL POPOLO
#PizzaTruck #AllGlass

On the approach, you'll be blinded by the sheer, shining beauty of this all-glass shipping container on wheels, tricked out with a wood-burning oven. While in line, you'll see people walking up and down the two levels of the truck like lemmings, throwing toppings on personal pizzas and firing them up in the oven until the crusts are charred. Getting a simple Margherita ($12) here will not disappoint, although adding a little meat ($3) to that sucker will kick it up to a new level.

DOTTIE'S TRUE BLUE CAFE
#pancakes #bacon #LongWait
28 6th Street

This place will test your patience like no other. No matter when you go, you'll stand in line in the shady part of town for enough time to go from hungry to raging, eat-your-arm hangry. The smell of bacon will hang over your head, torturing you the entire time. But stay strong and your wait will be rewarded with impossibly fluffy pancakes, delicious cornbread (with jalapeño jam!), and a crispy pile of bacon, all served in a beautiful, exposed-brick dining room by waiters who'll bring you back from the brink of starvation with a smile.

FARMERBROWN'S LITTLE SKILLET
#window #ChickenAndWaffles
360 Ritch Street

There is a little blue window on the side of a big brick building and it whispers sweet nothings into the afternoon air, beckoning you to come sample its juicy fried chicken and fluffy waffles. If you don't like your chicken on the fly, Farmerbrown's also offers a sit-down (but order at the counter) experience where they'll fill your metal tray with as much chicken as you'd like, and two perfectly square waffles with syrup. The adjacent bar serves tasty cocktails if you like to drown your bird in booze.

HONGRY KONG TRUCK
#HKStreetFood #EggTarts

Hong Kong is a place that's already a fusion of East and West, and Hongry Kong brings the best of both worlds to the streets. This food is wacky and mighty tasty, with a fun touch of DIY. You step up to the plate to create your own fusion dish by first selecting a sauce base, adding a protein, and then picking a starch (rice or spaghetti) to carry the flavor. All entrées are $9 and you can make them as American or Chinese as you'd like. For dessert, their custardy egg tarts are on par with anything in Chinatown.

HRD COFFEE SHOP
#KoreanBurritos #UniqueDiner
#ReallyNicePeeps
521A 3rd Street

Behind the faded HRD COFFEE SHOP sign on the window is a truly unique place. The décor is all diner, with red stools, ketchup trays, and a stray oldies song on the radio (which turns to MJ or Pharrell pretty quickly). But this diner serves Korean food. That's right; spicy, delicious, homemade gochujang is smothered on most of their menu items. The open kitchen is tiny but mighty, with five to six cooks bustin' out katsu, rice bowls, airy fries, luscious po boys, and surprisingly fantastic salads (with kiwi vinaigrette!). Even though they're a "diner," they never skimp on presentation and the vibe here is always homey. Their motto—"Good eats, nice peeps, grab a seat"—sums up the place best, plus you can get a coke if you so damn please.

MARKET & RYE
#brunch #PotreroHill
#ChickenSandwich
300 De Haro Street

Plan a casual Potrero brunch at this place, which serves amped-up brunch favorites and an incredible, cornflake-crusted chicken sandwich. The crunch of the chicken, paired with tangy slaw on a brioche bun, will drive you mad. You will not share this sandwich. You order at the counter, sit outside, and make fun of everybody who's likely still waiting in line for their brunch at more packed places.

FUN FACT

Chef/owner Ryan Scott also owns Mason next door and opened both restaurants simultaneously because he's nuts (and super talented).

MARLOWE
#GourmetBurger #TreatYourself
500 Brannan Street

A romantic place to get burger drippings on your elbows, Marlowe is a dark, chic corner spot that's great for a date. The other stuff on the menu, especially the bone marrow app, are amazing. But trust us, this $16 burger with a little lamb ground inside, cooked to a perfect medium rare, topped with bacon and slathered in horseradish aioli, will get you laid.

SAMOVAR TEA LOUNGE
#TeaService #DowntownViews
730 Howard Street

Samovar has several locations in the city, but

this one is right in the middle of Yerba Buena Gardens and offers mid-city views. You come to be both a lady and a (healthy) glutton. Samovar, which is Russian for "teapot," specializes in internationally inspired tea service. You can get the classic English version with a tiered platter of scones, jam, cream, and quiche, but they also have more creative offerings, like the Russian, Japanese, and Indian services ($20–$25). If you're the type who believes our predecessors (who are all dead, by the way) knew best, you can get the carbless Paleolithic service. Their tea selection is fantastic, the atmosphere skews business-casual during weekday lunch, and the dressed-up servers are light on their toes.

STREET FOOD PARK
#StreetTruckHeaven #OutdoorProjector #beer
428 11th Street

Wedged under a freeway, you'll find a gathering of fenced-in food trucks, huge projector screens, beer, coffee, and games with ample, cozy seating. A trailer park of the best kind, every food truck in here is street food royalty. Try a little something from everyone. Start with Filipino fusion sensation Señor Sisig, settle into their outdoor patio (or a school bus), play some skee ball, watch the game, and sip on a Blue Bottle pour-over from thrown-together Astronaut Cafe in the corner.

THE BUTLER & THE CHEF
#French #brunch
155A South Park

SOMA's South Park is a place Kenny would be proud to die, and his last brunch would be at this little French bistro, tucked into the corner and shaded by the park's many trees. The décor is colorful and the vibe is French casual. They serve croques, omelets, and *pan pardieu* and build their Salmon Eggs Benedict on French bread. Just when you think you're done Frenching, they sneak you a free truffle with your bill.

TONY BALONEY'S
#deli #lunch
1098 Howard Street

Tony has been slinging his baloney for twenty years and is a local lunch legend. This is a regular corner store, but their deli counter puts together fantastic sandwiches, salads (potato and pasta are the best), and prepared foods like lasagna. Tony and crew are the best and there is plenty of seating inside.

ZERO ZERO
#TreatYourself #pizza #cocktails
826 Folsom Street

Like pizza that grew up and got an MBA in tasty, Zero Zero (named after the flour used in their pizza dough) is an elegant place with tall windows, quirky but classy décor, a big wood-burning oven, and a balcony-level dining room. Their food is focused and refined without being pretentious. The pizza menu is filled with odes to SF streets, and the Fillmore, with its umami blast combo of hen of the woods mushrooms and pungent cheeses, is fantastic. The tiny gnocchi are fluffy, the composed salads hit every flavor note, and their cocktails are a must.

SEE AND DO

1AM
#graffiti #TinyExhibit
1000 Howard Street

At the end of the sketchiest block in SF, your eye will be drawn to the colorful mural on the side of 1AM's gallery. Dedicated to the history, culture, and appreciation of graffiti art, 1AM (shorthand for "1st Amendment") puts on classes and exhibits without getting too scholarly on the topic. The friendly people who run it are artists themselves, and you'll often find them working on graf projects in their side room. Check out their annual exhibit, "Honey, I Shrunk the Streets," where outdoor elements like trucks and dumpsters are miniaturized and sent to artists (like RWK) around the world who paint them up and return them to the gallery for a tiny exhibit that showcases an interesting collage of the world's street art.

OTP Tip: 1AM also hosts graffiti tours, where they'll take you around town for three hours for $50.

AT&T PARK
#Giants #FreeViewing
24 Willie Mays Plaza

SF's premiere baseball stadium, this huge structure sits right on the water and is a spectacle even on off days. Giants fans gather from far and wide in loud, orange-and-black masses to support their team, and if you'd like to be part of the pack, this stadium has an interesting feature that lets you watch some of the game for free. A viewing area is set up on the boardwalk in the back, where you get a wristband and can watch three innings for free (twenty-four people allowed per viewing period). If you do make it inside, there are lots of seafood-centric dining options, and if you want to catch your own damn dinner there's a fishing pier near the Marina entrance. Walking around the stadium is a cool way to explore the history of SF baseball, with statues of famous players like Willie Mays and Barry Bonds scattered about.

BAY TO BREAKERS
#naked #drunk #run
600 Townsend Street

An expression of SF's unique populace, Bay to Breakers kicks off every May to celebrate the city by rounding up almost everybody with feet and encouraging them to run from the Bay (Embarcadero) to the Breakers (12K away at the Pacific Ocean). The protocol here is to dress up like it's Halloween all over again (or just get naked), slowly jog for a while, and then get drunk and (respectfully) stupid at the after party.

HOW to Not Get Stabbed in SF

While San Franciscans are generally a peaceful, patchouli-toting bunch, we've discovered a few ways to get under their skin.

GOOGLE GLASS ON THE BART
Tech geek tensions are high, and sporting your glass puts you in the thick of it. Part with your gadgets to enjoy the city with your actual eyes and to avoid unnecessary drama.

SIXTH STREET
Sixth Street, between Market and Bryant Streets, is known as the most run-down part of the city. Here, many people live on the streets and not everybody is in touch with reality. What's crazy is that just one block over in any direction you'll find yuppies, cocktail bars, and tasting menus. Similar situations exist on stretches of nearby Turk, Eddy, and Ellis Streets above Market.

BURRITO VIOLENCE
Nobody will ever stab you for a burrito, well, maybe not. But there is a security guard at Pancho Villa Taqueria just in case things get out of hand.

DISS THE BURN
Burning Man is a serious topic around these parts; you'd better be wearing protective gear if you ever decide to tell a burner that BM is just an excuse to get high.

CARTOON ART MUSEUM
#museum #comics #GiftShop
655 Mission Street

Come here on the first Tuesday of the month when it's pay what you wish. You'll feel like it's Saturday morning with cartoons all over the walls, fun video exhibits on the projector, and an awesome gift shop that carries a variety of comics. The permanent exhibit is an excellent retrospective of the history of comics that features *New Yorker* cartoons, original *Garfield* strips with notes, *Calvin and Hobbes* lithographs, and *Felix the Cat* tone boards. The other three exhibit rooms always have something interesting on display and often focus on individual artists, flesh out the art of current animated films, or feature throwback cartoons. We saw the Ninja Turtles' exhibit here; turtle power!

FOLSOM STREET FAIR
#PublicS&M #SoMuchLeather
Folsom Street from 6th to 14th Streets

An expression of sexual freedom, every September, SF puts on an outdoor kink party where you'll be privy to eight blocks of leather-bound butts, public spanking, and dudes with dildo tails that wiggle when they walk. A total S&M shitshow, the Folsom Street Fair is not for the squeamish; fishnet body-suited fest-goers pop out of every alley, surprising you with their tits and bits. Expect massive crowds at all the local gay bars.

OTP Tip: The most popular getup is ass-less chaps, a leather harness, leather hat, and a well-manicured black beard.

SEVENTH SON TATTOO
#LoftSpace #custom #color
65 Langton Street

A huge, open, first-floor loft on a tiny residential street, Seventh Son Tattoo has a gorgeous design, which translates into the tattoo work of the talented artists here. Before it's time to break skin, you can chill on their big, comfy couches to calm your nerves and listen to the constant buzz in the air. Come here for large custom pieces and color work. While they welcome walk-ins, appointments are highly recommended.

YERBA BUENA GARDENS
#MultiPurposeComplex #nerds
745 Mission Street

A pastel-colored complex that takes up several blocks and looks like a high school from afar, Yerba Buena Gardens has just about everything you can imagine, from a food court to a carousel and a water fountain to a skating rink. Yerba Buena features many courtyards with lots of things to see and a mid-level view of the city. Know that when nerdy conventions come to town, this place swarms with nerd herds who walk around like mad cows in every direction.

SHOP

Out of the Closet

OUT OF THE CLOSET
#JunkHunt #cheap
1295 Folsom Street

It may look like some postapocalyptic junk store upon entry, but don't be deterred. While their selection is spotty and the two-story space is mostly filled with empty racks and sparsely placed furniture, you'll find really big diamonds in this riffraff rough. Follow the sign upstairs past the shitty over-worn shoes and your dig will uncover brands like Free People, Calvin Klein, Banana Republic, and J Crew, all for shockingly low prices.

SF FOGG
#SmokeShop #HelpfulStaff
211 12th Street

Many smoke shops in SF feel like an exclusive gym, where you walk in and people check you out but can't be bothered with your presence. SF FOGG is different. A smoke shop where the staff is equal parts friendly and high as fuck, this place carries everything to feed your smoking needs. A cool thing you can pick up here is the Bumble Bee ($30), a vape cig loaded with hash oil that'll last you one hundred good hits.

WORKSHOP RESIDENCE
#ArtMerch #ToteBag #Dogpatch
833 22nd Street

The Workshop is a space where artists hooked up with textile makers, who then hooked up with designers and producers to make art come to life. They sell everything from totes to sailboats and support different projects, so inventory is constantly changing. The popular thing here is a tote bag designed to look like a plastic "Thank You" bag. At $28, it will be the most expensive shit bag you'll ever buy, but it's a memento from the state that was the first to ban plastic bags.

PARTYING

21ST AMENDMENT BREWERY
#brewery #bar #BeerWithStyle
563 2nd Street

We appreciate a well-designed beer label, and 21st Amendment gives their home brews special design treatment. Each beer they put out is unique in both flavor and aesthetic, with colorful pictures that wrap around each can. They brew seasonal beers in quirky flavors like watermelon. While you can get the labor of their love at many stores and bars around the city, their SOMA bar is a collection of bests in a loud and fun atmosphere, with lots of seating and delicious food.

ALCHEMIST BAR & LOUNGE
#DestinationCocktails #CoolDécor
679 3rd Street

This is a serious mixology lounge with a blacked-out entrance and flickering wrought-iron sconces that'll put you in the mood for some fancy cocktails. Alchemist has a speakeasy feel, with multiple levels all decked out with exposed brick, classy leather couches, interesting sculptures and light fixtures, and old films projected behind the bar. Their list of cocktails is short and every drink is a masterpiece of balanced flavors, with a house cocktail that changes every Tuesday.

ALIBI THE PINK ELEPHANT
#DIYMimosas #GetSloppyOnChampagne
142 Minna Street

Located in an alley, the Delirium pink elephant guides the way, but you'll only have yourself to blame for getting shwasted here. Eat a hearty breakfast, then come here to take advantage of their mimosa setup, where they (dangerously) put the drink mixing in your hands. For $18, you get to make your own mimosa, using their twenty varieties of mixers placed on the bar in boots. Flavors include just about anything you can juice, like watermelon, carrot, and hot jalapeño, or you can sip on straight bubbles if you're not trying to mess with a good thing.

ANCHOR BREWING COMPANY
#FreeBeer #BreweryTour
1705 Mariposa Street

This is a historic brewery that's been honing its craft since 1849. San Franciscans down Anchor Steam like it's angel tears. For $15, not only do you get an extensive tour of the brewery, they'll sit you down in a private taproom and pour a handful of different beers into your eager chalice. Some are widely available, while others come with "I've had it and you didn't" bragging rights. Make sure to reserve your spot a few weeks in advance.

BLOOMS SALOON
#OldCrowd #AwesomeView
1318 18th Street

At the top of Potrero sits a dusty saloon packed with lots of old men, some pretty crappy beer, and odd music. But at the back of Blooms, there is one giant window that gives you a picture-postcard aerial view of downtown SF that you'll never forget. Sip on that Bud Light slowly, take in the putrid smell of Fixodent, and know that your eyes are being treated to a little bit of hidden magic.

BOTTOM OF THE HILL
#LiveMusic #intimate
1233 17th Street

Bottom of the Hill is a small bar with a blue-lit stage in the back that puts on fun shows. They choose bands that sound good up close and covers range between $8 and $12. Some shows are the types where your roommate's friend of a friend is playing; others feature bands that are just starting to gain steam, with a handful of bigger (but not huge) names on the calendar as well. An all-around good place to get sweaty with strangers, Bottom of the Hill is consistently recognized as a top venue in SF.

BRAINWASH CAFE & LAUNDROMAT
#coffee #OpenMic #CleanPanties
1122 Folsom Street

Like the Disneyland of laundry, BrainWash has beer, coffee, food, a solid social scene, an arcade (with Dirty Harry pinball), WiFi, and plenty of outlets. They've done everything in their power to make laundry day less of a chore, and you don't even have to throw in a load to have a fun time. They host open mics, comedy shows, and live music almost every night, and everything smells like dryer sheets.

CELLARMAKER BREWING CO.
#microbrewery #growlers
1150 Howard Street

Cellarmaker is housed in an obscure black building; the inside is exposed brick with wood paneling enclosing the front. It looks mysterious enough to entice you to go in, and there's so much beer in there you'll never come out. Cellarmaker is a microbrewery sticking its foot into the SF brew scene with some ballsy beer. They like experimenting with crazy brew methods and giving their creations quirky names like Coffee and

Cigarettes. You can try anything on tap in a number of ways: five-ounce tastings, half and full pints, liter bottles, and growlers to go.

CITY BEER STORE
#store #bar
1168 Folsom Street

At City Beer Store you have some serious decisions to make. Both a store and a bar, you first pick your brew from the many bottles they sell, then you can either take it to go or consume your bounty at the subterranean bar. The dollar corking fee still makes it cheaper than your average bar, but the selection is huge, the atmosphere is relaxed, and the beers on tap add a few more choices to the mix.

DRIFTWOOD BAR
#BYOVinyl #ClassyCocktails
1225 Folsom Street

Boasting "earthy beats and dusty glasses," Driftwood is a comfy, nautical cocktail lounge that encourages you to bring your own vinyl, which they'll pop onto the record player (if it's worthy, that is). There's a piano and a fireplace, and while Driftwood feels a little *Anchorman*, their short list of refined cocktails ($9 each) are no joke.

F8
#DanceClub #StaminaSundays
1192 Folsom Street

A nonpretentious club with lots of fun dance nights, F8 has something to move you every night. Stamina Sundays is a weekly event that'll pump free drum and bass through your brunch-battered bones. To keep your dance mojo on max, they run drink specials on most nights, where drafts are a measly $3 and wells are two for one.

FOLSOM STREET FOUNDRY
#hidden #games
1425 Folsom Street

Behind a blacked-out front that's really easy to miss, you'll find a game wonderland warehouse bursting with big screens so you can perfect your Mario Kart skills while everyone watches. If you're more of a throwback gamer, there are board games and cards to satisfy your retro soul. They put on tournaments, hold various game nights (Tuesdays), fashion shows, and nerd gatherings of all sorts. Their cocktails aren't stellar, but beers are $5 and beer pong is on the menu, too.

LOCAL EDITION
#CultCocktails #VintageTypewriters
#UnderTheHearst
691 Market Street

Cocktails are an important part of the SF drinking culture, and every new cocktail place is first compared to Local Edition, the bar that sets the bar for other bars. These mixology superstars practice their craft in an expansive, subterranean, newspaper-inspired bar that sits beneath the Hearst building, a historical landmark and former home of the *San Francisco Examiner*. Put on your most elegant shoes, order the Chief, a strong whiskey-based cocktail in a highball, and settle in near a vintage typewriter for the full effect.

SLIM'S
#LiveMusic #BigBands
333 11th Street

A bigger venue, Slim's first opened in 1988 and puts on bigger names and fun throwbacks like Blind Melon. This is a two-story venue, and you have the option of tacking about $20 on the show ticket price for a prix fixe dinner, which grants you early admission and a seat with a solid view of the stage from the balcony. We like to get down in the pit, but it's nice to have the option of resting your party legs.

FUN FACT

Slim's spent over $250,000 on soundproofing to shut up the next-door neighbor who complains about the noise. She still calls the police, but they ignore her.

SOUTHSIDE SPIRIT HOUSE
#CoolDécor #FreePizza
575 Howard Street

Many bars put on gimmicks to get people drinking on the weekdays, but Southside bumps it up a notch by offering the best deal in town (and on Saturday!): For every two drinks you order, they slip you a free pizza. They have creative décor that includes a wall of old cassettes and the atmosphere is lively. If you're really livin', Southside offers the Gamut, a $25 package that includes a can of Hamm's, tater tots, and pizza, plus a perfect finishing shot of Fernet.

TEMPEST
#SuperDive #GreatFood
431 Natoma Street

To take a breather from fancy cocktails, hit the Tempest, a charming super dive. Lube up with a shot of Jameson and PBR ($5), get a round of pool or Street Fighter under your belt, enjoy the slightly raunchy wall art, and lounge in this brick box until hunger strikes. Don't let the grimy bathroom fool you; Tempest serves amazing burgers and fries, which act as a perfect belly cradle for their cheap drinks.

THIRD RAIL
#cocktails #jerky #Dogpatch
628 20th Street

According to Third Rail, the best complement to your tasty cocktail is jerky, made in-house by jerky master Phil West, who marinades and dries the meat to perfection. All the jerky selections, which include a vegetarian option, offer a unique punch of flavor and spice sold by the ounce ($2.50–$4), and are served on butcher paper alongside your equally amazing cocktail ($10). The décor is industrial but cozy, and if you need a smoke after your jerky and booze, the view from outside is of a dilapidated steel company.

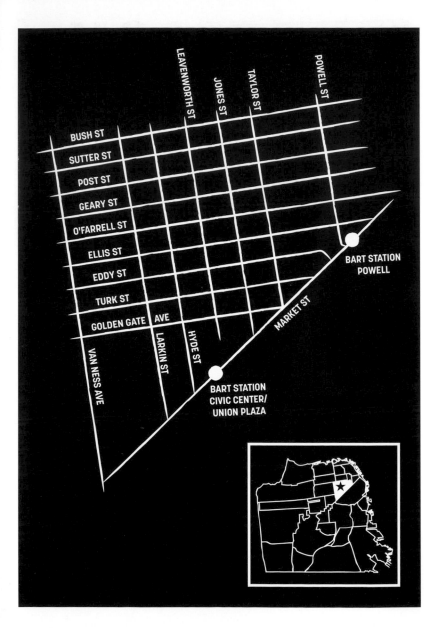

TENDERLOIN/ UNION SQUARE/ CIVIC CENTER

The Tenderloin was never a butcher's town nor a place where meat had any significance. It was, and to some extent, still is, a bit on the seedy side. Flanked by the Union Square and Civic Center touristy business districts, the Tenderloin is where post–Gold Rush red-light districts thrived, prohibition speakeasies flourished, and the occasional steak was eaten. Nowadays, the Loin maintains its grime but has fancier cocktail lounges, like the infamous Bourbon & Branch. As dirty as it may sound, if you go far enough uphill you'll end up in Tendernob, a cleaned-up microhood rubbing loins with Nob Hill.

☕ COFFEE AND BAKERIES

BEANSTALK CAFE
#tiny #ToastCups
724 Bush Street

BeanStalk is a really tiny place, made smaller by the owner's friends hanging out and taking up the very limited seating. But you're not here to sit. BeanStalk prepares a brilliant portable breakfast that consists of toast laid out in muffin tins, filled with a layer of bacon and an egg, then baked until golden. Their espresso comes in microscopic mason jars, and their cookies, cakes, and bars are equally adorable.

FARM:TABLE
#coffee #breakfast
754 Post Street

With a small, focused breakfast menu to match the tiny shop, farm:table offers only a few things, but each is so carefully and lovingly prepared you won't need any more options. Their daily toast with rotating toppings is always terrific and comes with savory or sweet ingredients piled high on top. The pastries are from Starter Bakery, and their croissant sandwiches are always a good bet. Finish off with a cappuccino and you're ready to take on bigger, but probably not better, things.

HOOKER'S SWEET TREATS
#caramel #Sightglass
754 Post Street

Nobody makes caramel the way Hooker's does, and this little shop sells this specialty in a number of ways. Have it drizzled over bread pudding, as a bar, or in solid candy form, mixed in with ingredients that accent the perfectly burnt sugar. Displayed in little crinkly candy papers, each caramel is handmade, and the chocolate-covered salted caramel, with a cup of smooth Sightglass coffee, is a flavor combination you'll fall in love with.

EAT

ANANDA FUARA
#vegetarian #Neatloaf #CultOperated
1298 Market Street

Ananda Fuara looks like a shithole from the outside but is clean—and creepy—inside. This place is run by some sort of cult (for real) and feels like stepping into a weird religious world of vegetarian food. The waitresses wear saris, there's no music, and there are awkward pictures of monks on the walls. Despite all that madness, they serve fresh salads and Indian-influenced dishes like chaat and dal. Their big-ticket item is the Neatloaf, which is a little weird in texture but comes with a perfectly tangy BBQ sauce. Bypass the overflowing shopping carts on Market Street to get to this cult of fresh veggie food.

COCO BANG
#Korean #DrunkFood #UnionSquare
550 Taylor Street

CoCo Bang is open until 4 a.m. on weekends so you can end your night with a Korean grease bomb. Firing on all cylinders, their spicy fried chicken will wake up your smelly mouth with a big hit of flavor. You can even order an entire chicken and have them spice it to whatever level you're craving. Their kimchi fried rice is wonderfully tangy and they do soju cocktails to keep the party going.

DE AFGHANAN KABOB HOUSE
#meat #rice
1035 Geary Street

De Afghanan is awkwardly sandwiched between two much larger buildings, and while it may look funny from the outside, nobody is laughing at the Afghani deliciousness that lives inside. If you're not familiar with this cuisine, don't be scared; most of the menu is just well-prepared meats, sauces, and rice. Seating is sparse, but the flavors are huge.

HYDE AWAY BLUES BBQ AND GUMBO CAFE
#BeefRibs #TinyHiddenSpace
457 Hyde Street

Look for a sign that says BBQ on Hyde Street and you'll find a tiny space cluttered with a bunch of knickknacks and chili peppers.

The sandwich board lists their daily meat offerings, and if you see beef ribs you're in for a food coma. Their buttermilk fried chicken rocks, the lobster mac is decadent, and the sides are simple but never disappoint. Eating here means getting your elbows in someone else's dinner, but you'll always leave with a smile and a new friend.

LERS ROS THAI
#FrogLegs #DateNight
730 Larkin Street

Part of a mini-chain of more upscale Thai, this location features weird meats like rabbit, frog legs, quail, and alligator. Their entrées aren't piled high like most Thai, but mindfully prepared and presented in fancier dishes with concentrated flavors. To start, try the frog legs, which come with roasted garlic chips on top. Their tofu and curry dishes may be small but they're filling. The prices are higher than usual and the spice levels are calibrated to American palates. It's the perfect place for a date, especially when you end it with their perfectly chewy and creamy mango sticky rice.

OTP Tip: They'll hook you up with free fried ice cream for birthdays, real or fake. Be warned: They turn down the lights and sing.

LITTLE GRIDDLE
#DoughnutBurgers #CivicCenter
1400 Market Street

This little griddle is churning out burgers that hurt. Huge and sinister, the Lucifer is the kind of ridiculous burger you see on lists of food items that'll kill you upon consumption. It's a bacon cheeseburger served between two glazed doughnuts that'll send your cholesterol straight to hell. You'll come out a guilty sinner covered in bacon grease and sugar glaze.

MORTY'S DELICATESSEN
#reuben #PeopleWatching
280 Golden Gate Avenue

A good deli sandwich is like a food hug, and Morty's will squeeze you tight and only let you go when you've almost stopped breathing. The reubens here are so flavorful, stuffed with moist pastrami (or corned beef, your choice) and Russian dressing oozing throughout, and best consumed on premises, where you can watch the crowd roll by through the window.

SAIGON SANDWICH
#BestBánhMì #SuperCheap
560 Larkin Street

Here's a fun game: Find a person in the food industry (a chef, a server, even a barista will do) and ask them about the best bánh mì they've ever had. Then watch them freak out as they tell you about Saigon, and offer to stop whatever they're doing to take you here. It's nothing more than a little shop filled with random packaged snacks and drinks, but the ladies here perform voodoo on these perfectly balanced sandwiches served on fresh, lightly crunchy bread. Plus, this little piece of heaven will cost you less than a latte.

SHOW DOGS
#WeirdMeats #CoolDécor
1020 Market Street

Show Dogs is a corner restaurant that looks like a train car with old Iron Maiden, Red Hot Chili Peppers, and other obscure show posters all over the walls. Their hot dogs are indeed show-worthy, with interesting meats like wild boar making the cut. They serve a variety of styles, including corn dogs and hot links, offer a super crispy fried chicken sandwich, and have excellent garlic cheese fries.

SWEET WOODRUFF
#FancyFood #CoolPresentations
798 Sutter Street

Dark and sexy with tall chalkboards, Sweet Woodruff will make sweet love to your mouth without screwing your wallet. Their dishes change frequently, but the menu usually features well-balanced sandwiches, hearty salads and soups, and amazing desserts, all presented on interesting service ware (which is sometimes a plate, other times a round of wood). The service gets slower at brunch, but their pancakes are worth the wait.

👁 SEE AND DO

ART PRIMO SF
#HiddenGraffitiGallery
#SprayCansSupplier
1124 Sutter Street

Art Primo's storefront is all whited-out with spray paint, making it blend in with the rest of the dilapidated buildings on the block. Once you find the door, you step right into the gallery space. This will be a little awkward, since the person sitting behind the counter is right there and the two of you will be sharing air without a word for a while. To break up the weirdness, get really focused on the art. They put on new exhibits every month, featuring new pop art. We walked in on the Bootleg Bart show, where artists reimagine Bart from *The Simpsons* doing various things like being eaten by Roseanne Bar(t). They also sell primo spray paint and graffiti supplies.

CITY HALL
#GorgeousBuilding #LawnShows
1 Dr. Carlton B. Goodlett Place

Many people come here to get married, renew their passports, and file paperwork.

You get to check it out for the sheer beauty of the building without all those chores. A huge, domed, majestic structure, City Hall has staircases and an inner rotunda that are spectacular. At night, you'll find various shows on its front lawn, including Giants games on the projector put on for the public.

GREAT AMERICAN MUSIC HALL
#DinnerAndAShow #landmark
859 O'Farrell Street

The oldest music venue in SF, this place hosts big-name concerts but still manages to feel intimate and friendly. The Great American Music Hall is best done as a dinner and show combo, which gets you up to the balcony for the show. Opened in 1907, the space is ornate with balconies and turn-of-the-century touches, but modernized with a kick-ass sound system and lighting. Until the Great Depression, this was a hot spot for gambling and "fast women." Today, the women are slower but the shows are just as exciting.

 # SHOP

HEART OF THE CITY FARMERS' MARKET

#HappyVendors
#CheaperThanFerryPlaza
1182 Market Street

This independent market is right off the Civic Center BART. It isn't huge, but it is much more manageable, cheaper, and open later than the one at Ferry Plaza. The vendors are personable, and you'll often find their kids working alongside them, bagging $2 kale and tiny tomatoes. Find the ridiculous egg guy so you can check out his chicken hat or the nut vendors where you can sample spicy wasabi pistachios by the handful. There's a little round-up of food trucks where you can get $5 pupusas, tamales, pie, and Indian food, among others.

YOU DOWN WITH POPOS?

POPOS are a beautiful thing. Privately Owned Public Spaces are scattered all around the city and include rooftops (or mid-level terraces) of the skyscrapers in downtown. These spaces are completely free to the public and are perfect spots to bring your lunch and admire the city views. We're not spilling all the beans, but an easy one to access is at One Kearny. Just walk up to the desk like you mean business and ask for the roof. There are a handful of others in the vicinity and discovering them will make you feel like a boss.

PARTYING

ACE'S
#GrandpasBar #KegTable
998 Sutter Street

This is an old-man dive with blue bar seats made of questionable material, where people come for game-day drinking and to watch old war vets shuffling around. Ace's is about kicking back a few with Gramps and loving it. The bros were saying something about a keg table, but we're too busy trading war stories to care.

BITTERS, BOCK & RYE
#whiskey #BBQ
1117 Polk Street

A three-part ordeal, Bitters, Bock & Rye is a taproom, a restaurant, and a lounge. You'll want to come here for their extensive selection of whiskey, and maybe a little BBQ to sweeten the deal. The smoky pulled pork pairs well with dark liquor, and a combo consists of two meats and two sides and will cost you $18.

FLY BAR & RESTAURANT
#CoolDécor #YoungDayDrinkers
1085 Sutter Street

A huge corner bar with bottle-cap paintings on one side and sexy surrealist ladies on canvas on the other, we wouldn't mind being a fly on these well-decorated walls. Fly Bar attracts a younger day-drinking crowd and happy hour gets you $6 "house creations," $5 pizzas, and $1 off drafts.

TRADITION
#UniqueMenu #ProhibitionCocktails
441 Jones Street

From the same guys as cocktail superstar Local Edition, this cocktail bar is all about preserving "traditions" of the Prohibition era by offering drinks of the times, split up into specific styles. Here, you can pick a cocktail that would have been served at a tiki bar; a speakeasy; or an Irish, English, or Scottish pub during Prohibition. They also offer a few carefully selected beers, if hard liquor isn't your lawbreaking drink of choice. The vibe here is a notch above casual, but the drink prices are still affordable ($7–$9).

OTP Tip: We think this bar is an excellent alternative to Bourbon & Branch, the over-hyped drinking complex in this neighborhood. We're not saying B&B isn't cool, but it gets a little pretentious and is way too crowded.

WHISKEY THIEVES
#whiskey #LocalsBar
839 Geary Street

You'll find whatever dark liquor you fancy on their spaced-out bar shelf display, and the bartenders will always recommend a fantastic whiskey when you're stumped. Once everyone has turned their whiskey neat into a big drunk mess, the locals congregate outside to chat with the doorman. There is a TV in there so, come game time, shit gets louder than an orgy of pelicans.

OWL TREE
#owls #cocktails
601 Post Street

This place is all owl-ed out. From the outside, the first thing you'll see is a pixelated gray-scale owl mural and owl sculptures watching over it. Inside, the seating comprises big, round, studded low stools and booths separated by owl-imprinted glass. Once you've had a few drinks, the owls start closing in a bit; don't look the scary taxidermied one in the eye, ever.

ROMPER ROOM
#CoolLights #LeopardLounge
25 Maiden Lane

From the name to the lighting to the ridiculous lounge upstairs, this place wants you to get your freak on. On most nights, the Romper Room is neon-lit, which should feel trashy but doesn't. The $12 cocktails are fantastic and made with inventive, fresh ingredients. When you get a little sauced, put some chapstick and head upstairs to the Leopard Lounge, a kitty-colored area where keeping it in your pants starts to become a real challenge.

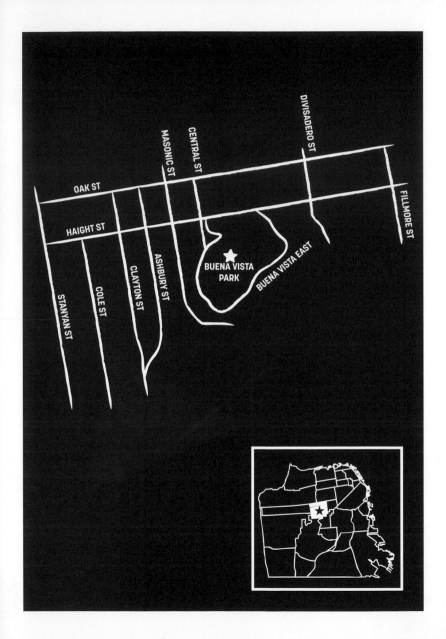

THE HAIGHT/ COLE VALLEY

The Haight was the epicenter of free love in the 1960s and the birthplace of the proper hippie. But as is the case with anything that gets mass public attention, the Haight has turned into a tourist attraction. People come here to take pictures of bohemian things, but ultimately spend money on the generic. If you want colorful bums, they're here, of all ages, races, and sanity levels. And people still smoke a bunch of weed, especially on Buena Vista Park's lawn and the hippie hill entrance to Golden Gate Park. Among the changing landscape, you'll still find traces of peace and love in the Haight's smaller cafés, hokey eateries, smoke shops, and certain thrift stores filled with tie-dye and Burning Man gear. Come as a conscious tourist and don't spend too long blocking traffic at the intersection of Haight and Ashbury.

COFFEE AND BAKERIES

CAFE DU SOLEIL
#coffee #pastries #LowerHaight
345 3rd Street

Cafe du Soleil is about as fancy as its name sounds, but with a good Haight grime layer over top. While their perfectly formed and displayed pastries would suggest otherwise, Soleil is not at all pretentious. They have long, rectangular tarts that you'll feel bad cutting, smooth pot de crème, and cheesy, crusted croque monsieur sandwiches. Come here for a coffee or a glass of wine, make use of the large sidewalk seating area, and admire the body-less heron mural on the side.

COFFEE TO THE PEOPLE
#Haight #hippies
1206 Masonic Avenue

As hippie as it gets when it comes to atmosphere, strangely, all of the baristas here are older Asian people. They've got dream catcher art, political quotes pasted onto tables, a big photo collage of Haight locals, a wall of world peace stickers, and a hideous orange-and-yellow color scheme. Their seasonal lattes, like pumpkin or gingerbread for the fall, are best enjoyed on their cuddle couches in the back.

FLYWHEEL COFFEE ROASTERS
#PourOvers #warehouse #Haight
672 Stanyan Street

A huge industrial-chic space with sassy design elements, Flywheel feels like an underground coffee party where the drinks of choice are delicious pour-overs. There's a roasting machine in the back, a barrel table with metal seats, all kinds of contraptions at the counter, lots of coffee cake loaves, and a backyard enclosed with wooden planks.

 # EAT

1428 HAIGHT
#crêpes #Haight
1428 Haight Street

Whether you're a people-watcher or want a private getaway, this casual breakfast joint has a full frontal window and a covered patio out back to serve all your seating needs. Their savory crêpes are stuffed to capacity and come with flavorful rosemary and garlic potatoes. On the sweeter side, they serve awesome stuffed French toast, waffles, and sweet crêpes. People gather in gaggles on weekends, so hit it Monday to Friday to avoid morning breath on your shoulder.

GREAT INDIAN FOOD
#Haight #CheapIndian #pizza
1793 Haight Street

The name is ballsy and they deliver on the promise. It's super janky, but their platters are cheap, well spiced, and filling. You pick your adventure from the lowboys to create a platter of stews, sides, and chutneys. This is a family-owned joint and the people here will make you feel welcome even if you're an Indian food noob. They also have $1.99 pizza slices and play Punjab music videos on the TV.

KATE'S KITCHEN
#brunch #FlannelHash #LowerHaight
471 Haight Street

Kate's will pull you out of that "drank too much," "spent too much" Saturday morning slump. The brunch here is dirt-cheap and their eggs are always perfectly poached. Start off with the hush puppies ($4.25) and slather those little pups with plenty of whipped butter. The best thing on the menu is the New England Flannel Hash ($10.50), a whole plate of corned beef and potato chunks with two eggs on top. It'll rescue you from the depths of hell, making you feel more human with every bite.

OTP Tip: Don't get sucked in by sexy words. The French Toast Orgy is mostly a giant pile of granola.

LOVE N HAIGHT DELI & CAFE
#lunch #VeganChickenAndSteak
#LowerHaight
553 Haight Street

Even though this is a dingy-looking deli with the word *vegetarian* haphazardly stuck to the front window, don't be afraid to pull the dangling doorknob. This place doesn't just open a pouch of tofurky and slap it on bread; Love N Haight offers all kinds of different "meats," from smoked chicken to pepper steak with ten different bread options. Each sandwich is $6-$7 and comes standard with sprouts, onions, lettuce, pickles, tomato, mustard, and mayo, and you can add avocado for 99 cents. There's a Buddhist shrine in the corner, a half-assed mural of Atlantis on the ceiling, and enough seating to plop down and eat your sandwich.

MAVEN
#FancyBarFood #cocktails #LowerHaight
598 Haight Street

Maven puts as much thought into their food as they do into their creative drinks, and the menu helps you pair the two seamlessly.

The décor is sleek and fresh. Fight for a seat upstairs and confidently order all the small plates with the cocktail pairings. Their shisito peppers rest on a sweet corn purée and are hit with a touch of maldon salt; the duck sliders are cleaned-up, Asian-spiced sloppy joes; and the mussels have a little Korean kick with absinthe worked into the delicious broth. Before you leave Maven, make sure to take a shot of Fernet, served in a tiny boot.

PADRECITO
#ColeValley #FancyMexican
901 Cole Street

Located in a pocket off the Haight called Cole Valley, Padrecito is a commanding sit-down, stay down, Mexican spot with big wooden booths and grown-up décor. While you can't argue with the beauty of a fat, cheap burrito, there is a different kind of delicious to be found here. From pork belly tacos to their delicate oxtail empanada, Padrecito brings it when it comes to flavor. Their tortillas are made fresh in-house, and while you'd be hard-pressed to find a Mexican in the dining room, the food is still authentic at the core, even with all the frills on top.

OTP Tip: This is better than nearby Nopalito, which aspires to be this good but hasn't quite nailed it.

PARADA 22
#Haight #PuertoRican
1805 Haight Street

Tourist-tested and Puerto Rican–approved, Parada 22 serves tostones, pernil, mofongo, and everything else your Latin-loving heart desires. To get you deeper into the island mood, good music is always on the radio and the prices ($10–$12 per entrée) won't kill the

good vibes. If you can push lunch late, all entrées drop down to only $6 during happy hour (Monday to Thursday, 4 to 6 p.m.).

PORK STORE CAFE
#HistoricDiner #VegFriendly #Haight
1451 Haight Street

In 1916, this place was a sausage store and butcher shop. Through the years, it morphed into a broad range of businesses (including a hair salon!), but has evolved into a breakfast restaurant. There's pork on the menu, but there's more than bacon to love here. They cook up eggs and throw them on a nest of shredded, fried potatoes and even have tofu scrambles for the veg heads.

RAGAZZA
#pizza #dinner
311 Divisadero Street

Ragazza is all the rave, and for good reason. A simply decorated place with a beautifully red-tiled counter and just one giant photo of several generations of Italian women on the wall, Ragazza serves equally focused pizza.

Their simple Margherita, with a paper-thin crust, zesty sauce, hand-pulled mozzarella, and a touch of basil, is phenomenal. If you want to get adventurous here, Ragazza melds things like chiles and pancetta into a spicy pie, and the Amatriciana ($18) is something you'll remember.

RICKYBOBBY
#BaconBurger #LowerHaight
400 Haight Street

A tiny space, Rickybobby has a small, always changing menu with bad-ass flair. Their beef bacon burger, where the two meats are ground and harmoniously cooked together, is a crowd-pleasing menu mainstay. Rickybobby has a deft hand when it comes to meat, especially with fancier cuts like prime rib. Pull out your favorite, all 'merican NASCAR jokes, and get elbow-deep in beef juice and pork fries.

ZAZIE
#brunch #patio
941 Cole Street

There is nothing you can do about the hour wait for brunch every weekend (except come on a weekday, when they serve the same brunch, those sly devils). So what's the fuss? For starters, you make your own mimosas by ordering a bottle of champagne (starting at $35) and your choice of mixer. Second, they serve perfectly poached eggs, tangy hollandaise, and sneak a little Dungeness crab into their Benedict Al Mer. Zazie's "miracle" pancakes are always amazing, and the Tahiti French toast—made with challah—is a fluffy culinary masterpiece. Here, you order by the piece, which means if you want one pancake and one slice of French toast, that's totally doable. Their patio is a spectacular place to enjoy your well-prepared brunch.

SEE AND DO

BEN & JERRY'S
#Haight #FamousCorner
#TouristIceCream
1480 Haight Street

While Ben & Jerry's started in Vermont, the corner of Haight and Ashbury is where the hippie ice cream magic exploded. So what can you get here that's not in the supermarket freezer aisle? For one, fresh-baked waffle cones. They also make big stoner sundaes, have special flavors, and their shakes are thick as fuck. If you've got $6 to throw at nostalgia, get a scoop of Cherry Garcia (also available in frozen yogurt).

BRAINDROPS
#piercing #UniqueJewelry
1324 Haight Street

Aside from having top-notch piercers and squeaky-clean equipment, Braindrops carries some of the coolest, most ornate body jewelry on the market. Their prices are already reasonable and they offer many discounts. Come in on your birthday for 13 percent off (free if it's your eighteenth), and if you buy piercings in bulk you'll save even

more. Every Tuesday from noon to 7 p.m., you can pop in here to get your teeth blinged out with rhinestones to make Lil' Wayne proud.

BUENA VISTA PARK
#Haight #PassedOutHippies #views
Haight Street and Buena Vista East

Buena Vista Park is pretty sketchy for the most part. Lying on the grass is usually reserved for the hippie homeless kids, and hiking up to the top may expose you to some intense local flavor (i.e., a dude pooping in the bush). If you choose to explore anyway, it's an uphill climb surrounded by trees, with many people taking casual jogs with their dogs. Up at the top, you'll get a view of the Haight and be in a perfect position to hike it out to the Castro.

🏪 SHOP

AMOEBA MUSIC
#legendary #records #Haight
1855 Haight Street

The grandmother of indie record stores, Amoeba still stands strong despite the digital times. The second store of the successful chain, this Amoeba was built in a converted bowling alley in 1997. It's colorful, a little worn-in, and filled with knowledgeable people who'll point you toward good music. Along with a huge selection of vinyl and collectibles, Amoeba puts on live shows in-store to keep the indie spirit alive.

BOUND TOGETHER ANARCHIST COLLECTIVE BOOKSTORE
#Haight #LeftyLiterature
1369 Haight Street

Run by a group of stick-it-to-the-man volunteers, Bound Together is a bit of flavor left over from the Haight's heyday. The store carries anarchist literature—mostly books and magazines—some written by inmates. There's a good amount of liberal propaganda covering the place, and if you come with an open mind you'll pick up a lot of information. It's a unique store dedicated to education and inspiring conversation about counterculture.

COSTUMES ON HAIGHT
#Halloween #accessories #LowerHaight
735 Haight Street

In San Francisco, feather boas and leopard-print unitards are a year-round necessity, and this store stocks whatever crazy things you need for Halloween or otherwise. Feel like your sister's wedding would be more fun if you looked like Ron Burgundy? Want to impress your OkCupid date with your ability to transform yourself into a unicorn? Come here, buy up all the mustaches and polyester, and donate your real clothes to charity.

GROOVE MERCHANTS RECORDS
#vinyl #small #LowerHaight
687 Haight Street

A jazzy record store that's clean, small, and easy to pick through, Groove Merchants isn't very touristy and it's a cool place to spend an hour digging. They sell a bunch of soul, funk,

carries morbid merch and is decked out in skeletons, taxidermy, and embalming tools. There's a lot of cool (but expensive) jewelry (some made from human hair and teeth), remains in jars, and baby skulls. You'll also find gifts, souvenirs, and housewares on the cheaper end of the spectrum. Upstairs, the gallery is filled with the kind of curiosities that'll make you feel dead all over. The shop appeared on the show *Oddities*, and attracts tourists as a result. They do not allow picture taking.

PIEDMONT BOUTIQUE
#feathers #neon #WindowLegs #Haight
1452 Haight Street

We're pretty sure Piedmont hoarded the entire world supply of stretchy, neon, sparkly fabric in the store. Under the Haight's iconic, fishnetted legs sculpture, you'll walk into this store vanilla and emerge covered in rainbows, feathers, and butterflies. They have endless walls of wigs, masks, pasties, booty shorts, and every pleather thing your little slutty heart desires. The prices are high, but the selection is unparalleled.

and hip-hop with a whole wall of 45s. The staff leaves you alone to browse, but if you need them they're around for suggestions and musical small talk.

HELD OVER
#Haight #RealVintage #MeatLocker
1543 Haight Street

Specializing in real vintage and retro fashions, this place has a whole rack of tiny Lederhosen, Bavarian dirndls, and peasant blouses. Sorted by decade, with weird stuff in every section, the merch at Held Over includes lots of leather, old party dresses, corsets, hats, and grungy T-shirts. The "Meat Locker" is a separate room for menswear, where you'll find buttoned-up retro styles. Plus, you can always count on them having a creative display window with mannequins engaging in some raunchy scenes up front.

LOVED TO DEATH
#WindowShop #oddities #Haight
1681 Haight Street

An "articulated gallery," Loved to Death

ROOKY RICARDO'S RECORDS
#VinylDig #ListenBeforeBuying #LowerHaight
448 Haight Street

It started over twenty-five years ago, when Dick came up on a truckload of 45s from an out-of-business distributor. Instead of letting them collect dust in the garage, he opened Rooky Ricardo's, a unique record store where you feel the love of music hit you upon entry. At Rooky's, you can pick up a funky record and listen to it in the store before making it yours. They carry a large selection of vinyl to leisurely browse, plus they often have record players for sale.

SUPER7

#Haight #NerdCentral #StarWars

1427 Haight Street

Super7 is filled with knickknacks for nerds, like *Star Wars* figurines, framed robot art, and exactly one Gameboy. About 80 percent of the store is dedicated to *Star Wars* in one way or another, and their quirky T-shirts run about $30. Beastie Boys will likely be on the radio when you come here to finally give in to your inner nerd.

URBAN AIR MARKET

#StreetFashion #music #ArtisanGoods #LowerHaight

An end-of-summer outdoor craft market with really amazing music, Urban Air Market features DJs playing actual records live, and the event quickly turns into a day dance party. What you will find here is an assortment of artisans selling jewelry, art, lots of SF-printed T-shirts, and Halloween costumes at the Goodwill stand ($8–$20). At the end of the market, by Pierce Street, you'll also find some shady Russians peddling weird-ass shit like sequin man thongs, tutus, rugs, and coats.

WASTELAND

#Haight #vintage #OldAndNewDesigner

1660 Haight Street

Wasteland is a pricier secondhand store, but it's like a supermarket of vintage finds. While some stuff is unfairly priced (e.g., Urban Outfitters tops at the same prices you'll find in-store), if you dig, older vintage threads can be found for a bargain. In the middle racks, there are new designer clothes that go for about $100 a piece. They also have shoes, boots, and really stylish accessories.

☺ | **PARTYING**

GOLD CANE COCKTAIL LOUNGE
#dive #Haight
1569 Haight Street

If you muster up the courage to get past the sketchy door at the Gold Cane, you'll realize that fear has probably kept you from some fun experiences. This place effectively repels tourists with its rough exterior and attracts a friendly neighborhood crowd with its gooey center of cheap beers, skilled bartenders, and rounds of pool. You'll earn a gold star just for going in, and a pimp cane for staying the night.

MOLOTOV'S
#dive #pinball #LowerHaight
1569 Haight Street

Molotov's is all about taking shots and getting shitty, usually with a dog or two underneath your feet. While there's a jukebox, the music will always be something loud and violent. Don't come here with any kind of service expectations; do come here for pinball, cheap drinks, and general debauchery. Keep your tourist card hidden.

NICKIES
#SportsBar #BottomlessBrunch #LowerHaight
466 Haight Street

Nickies offers a few things that keep us coming back, even though it's a football bar that gets fairly douchey on game days. First, their beer is fresher and bubblier than most, thanks to their glycol beer-dispensing system in the basement. Second, you get $8 bottomless mimosas with any brunch entrée.

You may get a TV tan with your buzz, but that's a hard deal to beat.

NOC NOC
#ColorfulCave #sake #LowerHaight
557 Haight Street

Less of a bar and more of a tripped-out cave that serves soft booze (i.e., sake, wine, and beer), Noc Noc has been around since 1986, playing strange techno and acid jazz before the cool kids caught on. The décor looks like a crazy caveman got his hands on some colorful paint, they serve affordable carafes of sake (hot or cold), and the music maintains a weirder-than-you're-comfortable-with edge.

THE ALEMBIC
#cocktails #FancyFood #SuperPopular
466 Haight Street

Every SF neighborhood has its fussy food and fancy cocktail lounge, and the Alembic fits that niche for the Haight. Eternally crowded, this bar serves things like bone marrow, pickled quail eggs, and offal prepared in ways that'll make you forget you're munching on a kidney. They don't do vodka sodas or Jäger shots; here, everything is carefully concocted, poured into proper glasses,

and garnished with a shaving of something or other. It may be too fancy for the hood, but their offerings are solid and fairly priced.

THE HOLY ROLLERS OF THE CHURCH OF 8 WHEELS
#RollerSkateChurchParty #LowerHaight
554 Fillmore Street

Practice your hallelujahs; we're taking you to church! The venue is a gutted church with a slippery skate floor, ankle-breaking rental skates, and a disco ball. This is what your parents did for fun and for $15, including skates. You can relive the good old days of skate-dancing to disco. Drink before you come, put on your booty shorts, and get in a *Boogie Nights* state of mind. Amen!

TORONADO
#IconicBeer #LowerHaight
547 Haight Street

Toronado is a beer pioneer and has been squeezing craft beer from its taps for well over twenty-five years. This isn't a hold-your-hand type establishment; you go into Toronado with a clear idea of what you want (check their site for brews on tap), pay with cash, and try to stay away from the word *artisanal*. It may come with a little attitude, but Toronado has earned its keep.

ZAM ZAM
#Haight #historic #martinis
1633 Haight Street

From the outside, Zam Zam looks like a haram. Inside, it's stuffy and musty, but makes you want to drink whatever the air has absorbed. The former watering hole of '60s hippie legends, Zam Zam opened in 1941 and was run by a guy named Bruno for fifty years. The drink here used to be the martini crafted by Bruno himself, who'd throw whatever he wanted in the glass. Come here to honor Bruno's memory and gather a half-century of stories from old regulars who refuse to go anywhere else.

Pacific Ocean

SEA CLIFF AVE

CLEMENT ST

GEARY BLVD

25TH AVE

20TH AVE

15TH AVE

10TH AVE

5TH AVE

ARGUELLO BLVD

BALBOA ST

FULTON ST

GG Park

THE RICHMOND

The Richmond runs along Golden Gate Park and is divided into Inner and Outer portions. Inner Richmond has a Chinatown comparable to the one in downtown, but here you can get your weird cheap vegetables and deer's legs without the photo op tourist roadblock. The crown jewels of the area are Burma Superstar, a place that serves a romaine-based salad that'll change your life, and Green Apple Books, a bookstore with a lot of charm. The further out into the Richmond you go, the better the dim sum gets. When you get to the Pacific Ocean, the Lands End trail is an eyeful of the scenic coastline.

☕ COFFEE AND BAKERIES

FIFTY/FIFTY
#RitualCoffee #DynamoDonuts
#InnerRichmond
3157 Geary Boulevard

Fifty serves the lethal combo of Dynamo doughnuts and Ritual coffee. Plus, they have perfect little muffins, freshly baked cookies, and salted caramel tea lattes. While the place is tiny, people still manage to squeeze laptops into every free space, including the bench set up in front of the bathroom to make the wait more comfortable.

GENKI CREPES & MINI-MART
#JapMerch #crêpes #InnerRichmond
330 Clement Street

This little market is filled with every weird Japanese candy, mochi variety, and bag of dried fish you've ever needed. Up front, the guys eagerly stand around to take your crêpe order, and once you've decided on your filling of choice and the accompanying

ice cream flavor, they put together a hand-held crêpe cone. The little bench outside is normally occupied by high school kids, but it's perfect for enjoying your cone of goodness.

HEARTBAKER
#bomboloni #InnerRichmond
1408 Clement Street

Jack Daniel's in bread pudding? Sounds like somebody's been listening in on our wildest dreams. Heartbaker's bread pudding selections change often, and while you may not always find this particular flavor, worry not; there's bomboloni to tide you over. Bombo-who-now? It's basically an Italian doughnut filled with flavored custard and Heartbaker makes it in several delicious varieties. They also have prepared sandwiches, salads, cakes, and charming window seating.

TOY BOAT DESSERT CAFE
#CoolDécor #cake #InnerRichmond
401 Clement Street

Stuck in a happy place circa 1960, Toy Boat is covered in the kind of nostalgia-inducing junk that'll make eating cake a fun outing. Swing past the rocket gumball machine and straight to the counter, where you'll be greeted by action figures, Pez dispensers, a faded picture of Fred Flintstone, and an assortment of cakes and desserts. Their New York cheesecake is the business, and the moist tiramisú with its amaretto-soaked bottom is not fucking around, either. The owner is peppy as can be and the cashiers will call you "dude" at least five times before you leave.

WING LEE BAKERY
#DimSumToGo #InnerRichmond
503 Clement Street

Don't get too mesmerized by the lady hanging over the big steel drums of dumplings and buns or jewel-like jellies and rice balls in the window. Place your order quickly, like you know what's up. Get a couple steamed buns, fluffy, filled with chicken or pork, and the size of your head; several 80-cent egg custards; and watch the lady throw everything in a bag and slide it across the counter to you. They (sort of) speak English but pointing will get you through.

EAT

BURMA SUPERSTAR
#Burmese #FamousFood
#InnerRichmond
309 Clement Street

A romaine-based lettuce salad is the most popular thing here, and it'll be one of your most memorable meals in San Francisco. You just have to trust us on this one. The place itself isn't anything great décor-wise, although the service is fantastic. Order the Tea Leaf Salad and the super-smiley server will bring it out unmixed and explain all the components. It will look like a pile of bird food and then she'll take a fork and spoon, squeeze the lemon, and mix it up for you. You will skept-ically take a bite of your ugly blackened salad and then understand. They fly out to Burma to get these tea leaves and ferment them forever, giving the salad a unique flavor that should be added as a sixth taste, right next to umami. Other menu items are just as good, and some come in little sizzling pots. Don't you dare leave here without trying that salad.

HALU
#yakitori #ramen #InnerRichmond
312 Eighth Avenue

If you're not a Beatles fan, the walls of this place will make you cringe. But we're here to eat ramen and not discuss Ringo. Halu is a family business and you feel it in both the service and the food. Start off with perfectly grilled meat on a stick, then move on to any one of their rich, flavorful bowls of ramen. Every component here, from meat to broth, is lovingly prepared and the vibe is homey and comforting.

HOT SAUCE AND PANKO
#HotWings #InnerRichmond
1545 Clement Street

This is the best place in San Francisco for chicken wings. People from far and wide make the pilgrimage here, and there are no less than twenty varieties of wings to choose from on any given day. They come in some creative flavors, like savory panko parm, bacon-wrapped bourbon molasses, sweet Kentucky-aki, and eye-burning ghost pepper wings. You can get a small (seven wings, $6.49) or a large (eleven wings, $9.89). Suck everything off those bones and come back for seconds.

O'MAI CAFE
#BloodAndTesticleSoup
#InnerRichmond
343 Clement Street

While the atmosphere here is updated and modern, with Vietnamese coffee served in mason jars, O'Mai doesn't shy away from throwing a few testicles and curdled blood into your soup, the way mom would. The Bun Bo Hue ($9.50) here is a masterpiece of animal parts steeped in a mildly flavored broth with veggie accompaniments. Another shining dish is the Kobe Carpaccio, or thinly sliced raw beef drizzled with fish sauce, spices, and crispy fried shallots. This one's costly at $11.50, but so worth it.

OTP Tip: "Pizzle" is code for Rocky Mountain Oysters, which is code for sheep balls.

PIZZETTA 211
#ThinCrustPizza #FreshIngredients
#OuterRichmond
211 23rd Avenue

This tiny little place pumps out some mighty fine "pizzettas," topped with seasonal ingredients in interesting combinations that karate chop every taste bud in your mouth. While the name makes you think you're getting a bite-sized little pizza, theirs are enough for a full lunch for one. Their menu is as small as their four-seater restaurant, with some items rotating biweekly. Luckily, you could (and should) get the rosemary, fiore sardo cheese, and pine nuts pizza every day.

RED A BAKERY
#Hawaiian #CheapEats #InnerRichmond
634 Clement Street

When's the last time you had spam? Red A is all about that canned meat treat and serves

it in a nori-rolled rice cube called musubi. We know it sounds gross, but they doctor up the spam and grill the mushy out of it to make it quite palatable. For something more substantial (and not out of a can), they serve huge Hawaiian teriyaki meat platters. Whatever you get here, you'll be in spam loving, old Chinese man company.

SHANGHAI DUMPLING KING
#Chinese #SoupDumplings
#OuterRichmond
3319 Balboa Street

This is real-deal dim sum. Their soupy XLB dumplings, hot and fresh, come with a delectable dipping sauce, the scallion pancakes are just perfect, and their pan-fried pork buns are crispy and delicious. Scan the menu, order as many things as you can afford the minute you sit down, and prepare to feel like dim sum royalty.

◉ SEE AND DO

LANDS END TRAIL
#EasyHike #AwesomeViews #SeaCliff

Lands End is a 3.4-mile cliffside trail with many interesting viewpoints. The trail itself isn't physically challenging, but it is very visually stimulating. It starts off touristy from the trailhead, but all the old people and slow walkers drop off quickly. Along the beachside cliff, you'll come across historic (but hard to see) shipwreck chunks in the ocean, beautiful redwoods whose leaves and branches have been hedged by the wind, and an amazing sand-pillowed stairway back down to the ocean at Mile Rock. Your best view of the Golden Gate is at the end of the trail near the ledge of the concentric circle rock sculpture. You'll see seals, seagulls, and sailboats, all with the backdrop of a seemingly impossible landscape.

SUTRO BATHS
#OceanView #landmark #SeaCliff
680 Point Lobos Avenue

Sutro Baths used to be a public bathhouse and indoor pool at the turn of the twentieth century. What remains of the Sutro Baths today are eerie ruins that are constantly being eaten by the ocean. You can climb into every part of the concrete chunks and balance on beams between grimy, tadpole-filled standing water, if you dare. There's also a cave. Once you poke your head in, your eyes will quickly adjust to the dark until the cave is punctured with a little naturally formed peephole where you can hear and see the ocean crashing through.

OTP Tip: Louis' is a small relic of a restaurant that's been hanging off the cliff overlooking Sutro Baths' remains since 1937. It's touristy, but it comes with an un-paralleled view.

🏪 SHOP

BLONDLOGIC
#thrift #CoolPricingGame
#InnerRichmond
792 Arguello Boulevard

A secondhand store tucked away by Golden Gate Park, here you'll find old H&M threads, weird out-of-style dresses, mom sweaters, BDG jeans hung neatly, bags, and strappy shoes. The selection at BlondLogic is just okay, but their resale process is the fun part. Based on the idea that things devalue over time, the highest price listed on the tag is from the day it was brought in. From that date, the price drops every month for two months until it is relegated to the 70-percent-off rack. If you find an item you love, you can either buy it on the spot or play the price game and wait for the date it goes on sale. If you've got no time for games, go straight to the 70-percent-off rack or check out their cheap jewelry collection at the counter.

GREEN APPLE BOOKS
#books #BetterGifts #NostalgiaCentral
#InnerRichmond
506 Clement Street

This multilevel bookstore is a special place that seems to have sidestepped the digital takeover. Split up into rooms named for apple varieties, this huge store carries all kinds of books, some annotated with little accurate and quirky descriptions. Each room houses different genres, and the Green Apple Room contains used bestsellers hidden on a shelf for only $5. Here, you'll find graffiti, "lowbrow" books, SF-specific literature, a large selection of cookbooks, and so much

more. The main area isn't just books, either, there are ridiculous printed patterns, things with Bill Murray on them, and our favorite—a "Baking with the Homies" set that includes cookie cutters shaped like 2PAC, Biggie, and EasyE. You'll hear employees shout over the loudspeaker and be transported to a time when the Internet was still called the World Wide Web.

PARK LIFE
#GadgetStore #InnerRichmond
220 Clement Street

Park Life sells the kind of stuff that would appear in *Paper Mag*, which they also sell. Cleanly designed, this store is a little pricey, but their merch is really interesting. The middle table is full of new books, like a collection of medical illustrations with watercolor drawings of diseases. Here, you'll find things like stencils, pencil sets, printed shirts, hoodies, hats, taco sandwich wallets, tiny magnets, and pocket monkeys. They also carry Herschel backpacks and similar brands in the back.

PARTYING

THE ABBEY TAVERN
#CollegeBar #FightNight
#InnerRichmond
4100 Geary Boulevard

Nine out of ten times, the Abbey is filled with bros and college students, but if there's a UFC fight going on, this is a good place to watch it. Other divey amenities include pool, darts, and $10 buckets of Bud. The sign on the side urges you to PARTY HERE; proceed with bro-watch caution.

OTP Tip: Need more TVs? Check out Ireland's 32 down the street, where they have TVs on top of TVs and a projector screen projecting a TV if all those TVs aren't enough for you.

THE BITTER END
#pub #DrunkFood #trivia
#InnerRichmond
441 Clement Street

This dive hosts the best trivia on Tuesdays and has a mixed grill plate with enough bacon and sausage to promote optimal brain function between cheap beers. Trivia nights here are very popular and coming early (around 8 p.m.) puts you in perfect position for both getting a seat and still catching the $2 draft happy hour. If you strike out at trivia early, there's a pool table and darts upstairs.

THE BLARNEY STONE
#Irish #sports #FreeGames
#OuterRichmond
5625 Geary Boulevard

An Irish pub that serves tater tots, cheap cocktails, has free air hockey, shuffleboard, and a huge backyard. They have several TVs and one giant projector screen, and the bartenders are really accommodating even when everyone is wasted. Come here on a weekend morning for greasy pub brunch, complete with a Bloody Mary, and don't worry about starting to drink too early; you'll be in good company.

THE HEARTH
#TrueDive #InnerRichmond
4701 Geary Boulevard

The Hearth isn't a destination bar, and few tourists make it out to this local dive. You'll have to respectfully find your seat among a slew of regulars, young and old. The Hearth is the kind of place where you'll hear someone ask, "Why the long face?" It's a place where the beers are cheap, the owner works the bar, and you'll watch people stumble away, one by one, to their respective homes a few blocks away.

THE PLOUGH AND STARS
#Irish #LiveMusic #InnerRichmond
116 Clement Street

Let the beer smells and Celtic sounds hit you on the way into the Plough and Stars, an Irish pub with soul. Their Guinness is thick and Irish accents fly around in the chatter. The bar puts on live music almost every night at 9 p.m. that'll feature at least one fiddle. It's an excellent spot to go for a few shots of Jameson, some loud Irish folk, and a long, drunken game of pool.

Golden Gate Park

The Golden Gate is an expansive park that sits between the Richmond and Sunset districts; it starts in the Haight and ends at the Pacific Ocean. William Hammond Hall designed it in the 1870s, transforming the land from a giant sand dune to a green wonderland, built in a similar style as (but 20 percent bigger than) New York's Central Park. Within these expansive grounds, you'll find a collection of activities and sights that'll keep you busy for days. These are a few of our favorite things.

FESTIVALS

THE OUTSIDE LANDS MUSIC AND ARTS FESTIVAL

Every August, the far end of the park turns into a food, wine, and music extravaganza, where every food truck, mom-and-pop shop, brewery, and winery rolls onto the green. In addition, the festival always puts on big-name acts like Radiohead, Arctic Monkeys, and Metallica. While tickets run about $100 per day for general admission (or $225 for a three-day pass), you'd spend a lot more on nosebleeds for some of these artists, and having access to every edible thing in the city doesn't hurt, either. Bring cash.

HARDLY STRICTLY BLUEGRASS FESTIVAL

The best free event in the city, Hardly Strictly comes to town in October and blows the roof off the park with six to seven stages and three days of loud, eclectic jams. As the name so covertly suggests, the festival isn't just about bluegrass, and artists like Deltron 3030, Yo La Tengo, and Sharon Van Etten share the stage with bearded dudes on ukuleles. Getting here by public transport (or cab/Uber/car) is very hard; you might want to bike it instead.

MUSEUMS

Two major museums can be found side by side in the park. Both are spectacular and you should visit them on two separate days to avoid desensitization.

DE YOUNG

A twisted, towering building located near the Japanese Tea Gardens, the de Young is an expansive fine art museum established in 1895. They always have something intriguing on display, whether it be political or just aesthetically pleasing in nature, and it holds a large permanent collection of fine American art. One of its best features is the observation deck, where you get a panoramic view of the city. General admission is $10 (free on the first Tuesday of the month), and special exhibits range from an additional $10–$25 each. The best time to hit it is on Friday night for their free after-hours party, where you'll get a little music and booze with your art.

OTP Tip: You get $2 off if you show them your Muni transfer, $1 off if you book online, and free admission if you've paid for the Legion of Honor (and vice versa).

CALIFORNIA ACADEMY OF SCIENCES

Everything you ever wanted to know about animals, plants, and ancient rock formations is here and best experienced Thursdays after dark. You'll want to look into every fish tank, pet the manta rays and starfish, dance to the EDM in the middle room, and watch the jellyfish pump to the beats. But before you do anything, you must go to the immersive rainforest exhibit. Line up before 7 p.m. and prepare to be mind-blown. You'll walk into a giant sphere at the bottom and progress through the ramps on the perimeter while butterflies and birds circle overhead.

Once you get to the canopy, the only way out is the elevator. They'll ask if you stole any butterflies, then shoot you down the elevator through the forest, and then below it into a tank with huge fish, a hungry anaconda, and other Amazonian sea life. From here, you have many paths to follow through the museum, but don't leave without seeing the Living Roof, a hobbit-like sanctuary atop the museum that always smells like BBQ. Entrance is $12 and you should bring an extra $20–$30 for drinks and food.

FUN FACT

The anaconda is fed frozen rabbits that are defrosted using a blow-dryer every time the snake gets hungry.

TREASURE HUNT

Golden Gate Park is best explored without a road map. Here are five gems we found within its depths.

HIPPIE HILL

Also lovingly referred to as "unemployment hill," this stretch of grass (on Stanyan and Kezer Streets) is full of really dirty kids. Some are voluntarily homeless, others are just hanging and everyone can sell you drugs; some will just take your money and run.

OTP Tip: A lot of homeless people on this side of the park live in trees. As such, your nature hike will sometimes feel like you walked into someone's living room.

HANDBALL COURTS

Somewhere off the trail, there are two indoor courts with tiny crawl-through doors and audience bleachers. These look like a super-creepy relic from the '70s.

CONSERVATORY OF FLOWERS

A whitewashed, castlelike structure, this conservatory has atriums with every kind of flower you can imagine inside. On weekends, musicians play in the tunnel on its pathway. Entrance is $8.

STOW LAKE

This human-made lake features paddle boats, ducks, waterfalls, picnic benches, and a Chinese pavilion with little stone stools built into the rotunda.

REDWOOD FOREST

Veer off JFK Road once the big trees appear. You'll feel like Little Red Riding Hood in this spectacular forest where only thin rays of light filter through the branches. It's eerily quiet and peaceful.

OTP Tip: If your feet get tired, there's a free shuttle along the length of the park (on JFK Road) that runs every fifteen minutes.

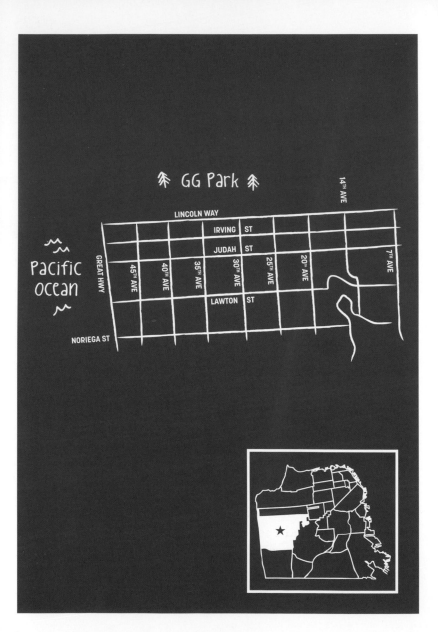

THE SUNSET

With more fog than sun, the Sunset is actually not a misnomer. Back when these lands were sand dunes, a smart businessman named the region something beautiful to get people interested. A shady move, but we're glad it created a boom in development because this neighborhood is fantastic. Buck up about the fog, because the Sunset is home to Arizmendi, the best focaccia bakery in the city, authentic Thai at Marnee, and a set of mind-blowing mosaic steps with a panoramic view at the top. The N Judah rail runs through the Sunset, which makes getting here not as hard as locals will tell you. It ends at the ocean, which is full of great white sharks.

☕ COFFEE AND BAKERIES

ANDYTOWN COFFEE ROASTERS
#SnowyPlover #cookies #OuterSunset
3655 Lawton Street

Andytown is like the café version of that girl in high school who never had a hair out of place. Their coffee, pastries, and clean atmosphere are all perfection. Their Snowy Plover, a mix of soda water, coffee, and whipped cream, is a ballsy and amazing specialty drink. They use wooden planks instead of plates to present their beautiful baked goods, like the cocoa nib chocolate heart cookie that's expertly hit with a bit of salt. It's all in the details here, and Andytown gets everything just right.

ARIZMENDI BAKERY
#focaccia #EmployeeOwned
#InnerSunset
1331 9th Avenue

A co-op bakery that first started in Berkeley and gained huge popularity across the bay. Since Arizmendi is employee-owned and run, there is no "man" waving a rolling pin. This gives them the flexibility to be creative and put extra love into everything they make. And, holy shit, can these guys put together a focaccia pizza and unique baked goods. Aside from everything tasting phenomenal, the good feelings will come from knowing that you're supporting a local business.

POLLY ANN ICE CREAM
#AsianIceCream #FlavorWheel
#OuterSunset
3138 Noriega Street

Should ice cream ever be black? Polly Ann

says yes, and their black sesame flavor is mighty tasty. Peddling Asian ice cream flavors for over fifty years, they've got your red bean, lychee, and the best damn green tea ice cream this side of Chinatown. Plus, you can spin the wheel of ice cream fortune that will pick a flavor for you if you're waffling around. Landed on funky as fuck durian? Tough nuts, toots.

SNOWBIRD COFFEE

#LikeACatalogCafé #CaféBombón
#InnerSunset
1352 A 9th Avenue

If you were to 3D-print the perfect coffee shop, this one would be it. Snowbird is hyper detail-oriented, and the shop is long, narrow, beautifully painted and wallpapered, and with plenty of crafty seating, including a hangout lounge with armchairs in the back. Their condiments hide in white, neat containers and the pour-over station is pro. The butcher-aproned baristas are pros at pulling creamy shots, but if you're in the market for some-thing with actual sweet dairy, they pop a bit of sweetened condensed milk into your espresso to make a café bombón.

TROUBLE COFFEE COMPANY

#BadassCoffee #OuterSunset
4033 Judah Street

Decked out in weird found items (like a naked plastic baby) and run by tatted baristas, Trouble has a good amount of 'tude. This bit of edge transfers to their menu, where you can get a "Build Your Own Damn House," a fresh coconut filled with its own delicious water, a coffee, and a huge, fluffy slice of cinnamon toast. Their menu looks like someone wrote it in detention and the interior seems to flow seamlessly into the outdoor seating area that's made up of impressive driftwood.

EAT

ART'S CAFE
**#KoreanDiner #HashbrownSandwiches
#InnerSunset**
747 Irving Street

Art's takes everything we love about American breakfast and fuses it with Korean favorites to create something truly unique. The Korean-American breakfast offerings include omelets stuffed with bibimbap and bulgogi hashbrown sandwiches, where crispy potatoes take the place of bread. Getting a seat here is going to be a total bitch, since it's just a narrow diner with stools. But there aren't many places where you can get kimchi with your eggs, so you'll have to wait it out.

DEVIL'S TEETH BAKING COMPANY
#beignets #breakfast #OuterSunset
3876 Noriega Street

From their couch cushion–sized cinnamon rolls to their $1 beignets (on Sundays) and doughnut muffins, nothing is just average at Devil's Teeth. They seem to get a big kick out of shocking you with their creations, but they never let innovation mess with flavor. Everything here, including their incredible breakfast sandwiches, is delicious and made with your mouth in mind. The lines get long on Sunday, but you won't find this level of bakery tomfoolery anywhere else.

IZAKAYA SOZAI
#yakitori #ramen #InnerSunset
1500 Irving Street

What's the best part of a chicken? The skin, obviously. This Izakaya knows what's up. They string up the skin on a stick and deep-fry that bad boy along with other speared items, like tender beef tongue, sardines, chicken hearts, and pork jowl. Also, they serve Tonkotsu Ramen ($9), a rich bowl of pork broth to which you can add succulent fried pork belly. Make a reservation here or you'll be smelling the waft of chicken skin and pig parts for an hour outside.

LIME TREE SOUTHEAST ASIAN KITCHEN
#CheapEats #curry #InnerSunset
450 Irving Street

Through a colorful entrance in the back of the building, you'll enter a bright green café that smells of sweet curry. Start off with the Roti Pratha, a warm, perfectly fried dough that comes with a flavorful curry dipping sauce. Continue the carb and curry journey with their Singaporean Curry Noodle, which is a heaping pile of glass noodles. All their dishes carry the distinct flavors of Indonesia (and surrounding countries) and for prices close to what you'd pay in Southeast Asia.

MANNA

#AuthenticKorean #DécorLess
#InnerSunset
845 Irving Street

Aside from being really bright, with one mirror on the wall and ugly rubber banded blinds, there is no ambience to speak of at Manna. But the little side dishes that fill up the tables and are served in different vessels are all the décor this place needs. Their food is authentic Korean BBQ fare, with things like sizzling spicy pork, bibimbap, and fantastic soups. While there are a lot of other faces there, actual Korean families eat at this joint, so you know it's legit.

MARNEE THAI

#AuthenticThai #AngelWings
#InnerAndOuterSunset
2225 Irving Street or 1243 9th Avenue

A Thai institution that's been around since 1986, Marnee knows a thing or two about Thai. The owner is from northern Thailand, and while many chefs have strayed into fusion, he chooses to keep things real and cooks his grandmother's recipes to the tee. Their garlic angel wings will make your Super Bowl Sunday bird parts taste bland, and the harmak, a fish-over-eggplant dish served in

a banana leaf, is so interesting your mouth won't know how to classify it. Their curries are rich and pungent and their meat is fall-apart tender. This is a family-style restaurant, and you should order a bunch of shit regardless of whether or not you intend to share it. Both locations are fantastic.

OUTERLANDS

#brunch #EggsInJail #OuterSunset
4001 Judah Street

We've all had pancakes and eggs for brunch, but not the way Outerlands makes them. Their pancakes are Dutch, which means that they're big buttery pies cooked in a cast-iron skillet with sweet or savory options to which you can add housemade ricotta. As for their eggs, they come in jail (two eggs hidden deep in a thick piece of toasted bread), Outerlands goes big with everything, including the décor, where you'll be surrounded by monstrous amounts of (reclaimed) wood with a majestic round bar and outdoor seating against a mosaic wall mural.

UNDERDOG

#OrganicHotDogs #VegDogs
1634 Irving Street

We always root for the underdog, especially if there are actual hot dogs involved. On the border of Outer and Inner Sunset lies a little shop with flavorful, do-gooder dogs. Their meats are all organic (or no meat at all for the veg heads), and their garlic sauce adds an herbaceous flavor. We're suckers for hot links and andouille, and Underdog does both justice. Feel free to reference their hot dog size chart to determine the right fit for you.

OTP Tip: Walk a few doors over for the Underdog Taco Shop (and margarita) experience.

👁 SEE AND DO

HIDDEN GARDEN STEPS

#StreetArt #views #OuterSunset
16th Avenue between Moraga and Noriega Streets

This is a colorful set of steps that features a mosaic illustrating the Earth from the ground to the sky. Financed and built in 2013 by the community around them, the vivid pictures on these steps start off with ground plants and unfold with every step to flower fields, jungles, and eventually the sky. You'll want to look down to get the full effect and will likely fall over your feet. Once at the top, the mural disappears and you're left with a panoramic, peaceful view of San Francisco on the horizon.

TUESDAY TATTOO

#HomeyShop #ArtyPros
4025 Judah Street

If the smell of the ocean inspires some ink, pop into Tuesday Tattoo and get that dolphin done right. Any day of the week—Jesse Tuesday, Hannah Wednesday, and Candi Kinyobi (that's "Friday" in Japanese)—will tat you up proper. Everyone here either holds a degree in art, has apprenticed in some of the best shops on the West Coast, or both. The shop is homey and welcoming, they won't judge your half-baked ideas, and their work is top-quality.

⊚ PARTYING

CHUG PUB
#DiveBar #BeerTower #OuterSunset
1849 Lincoln Way

You might as well pop those aspirin before you walk through Chug Pub's door. They have a beer tower and we don't advise that you take on this $35 beast alone; it will hurt you. The tower is a tabletop, three-liter tap, and they throw in a free side to slow your roll. The atmosphere is sporty, and if you're down a whole beer tower, it's also probably blurry.

DURTY NELLY'S
#SportsDive #Irish #OuterSunset
2328 Irving Street

A down-home Irish pub with perfect greasy bits, like fried sausages, to absorb all the durty drinking you'll be doing. They've got five TVs, so game-day madness is a given. The Sunset has its own flavor of sports fan, and they're mostly cheery old dudes. Every bartender here breaks a sweat when it's busy, so you'll never have to wait long for your perfectly poured Guinness.

FLANAHAN'S PUB
#dive #EverythingGoes #Irish
#OuterSunset
3805 Noriega Street

Walking through the green door at Flanahan's, you never know what you'll find. They'll randomly give out free hot dogs or have tacos on Tuesdays. One thing is for sure: This is an Irish spot where just about anything goes, filled to the brim with regular drunks and good times. Like throwing sharp objects in the dark? Flanahan's dartboard is your highway to drunk injuries.

THE LITTLE SHAMROCK
#BoardGames #OldSchoolDive
#InnerSunset
807 Lincoln Way

The Little Shamrock is right across from Golden Gate Park and is a divey pub to drink and play board games. The games are all torn up, but who doesn't love a round of drunken Jenga? There are also backgammon tables, lots of TVs, and an old-school jukebox filled with flip-through old tunes. This place has a lot of charm, $4 beers, and the kind of smell you can't quite put your finger on.

DAY TRIPS

San Francisco is an incredible city, but you can't ignore the whispers of the California coast. This area of the country is filled with diverse day trip possibilities. Just taking the BART across the bay to Oakland and Berkeley will give you a whole new perspective on the Bay Area. From world-famous wineries to snow-capped mountains, boat communities to Burning Man, having San Francisco as your starting point is something you should take advantage of.

OAKLAND

The high rents in San Francisco have driven many young professionals and creatives across the bay to Oakland. To get there, just hop on the BART, get off at 12th Street, and you'll be right in the heart of downtown. From there, you can explore the restaurants and bars on the strip and walk down to Lake Merritt for a peaceful retreat. The first Friday of the month, this stretch explodes into an art walk with awesome food and music. While not all of Oakland is happy fun times, stick to the west and north (like Temescal and Piedmont) and you'll be just fine.

BERKELEY

The ultimate college town, Berkeley is filled with young, eco-minded people (and some older hippies), and there's a lot to do, especially around the UC Berkeley campus. The "Gourmet Ghetto" along Shattuck Avenue between Rose and Delaware Streets is where California cuisine, in all its farm-to-table, organic, local, and sustainable glory, was born. The first Peet's Coffee opened here in 1966 and iconic Chez Panisse kickstarted the careers of many California chefs. Down on Telegraph Avenue, you'll find some of the highest, homeless hippies you've ever seen, cool shops—like the original Amoeba Music—cafés, and bars. We won't blame you if you miss the last BART to SF on Saturday night, and if you do, hit up Wat Mongkolratanaram, a Thai Buddhist temple that serves an amazing, dirt-cheap brunch from 10 a.m. to 1 p.m.

WINE COUNTRY

The wine produced in northern California is America's favorite way to stick it to the Italians. Taking a trip to Napa, Sonoma, or Mendocino is a welcome departure from hopping from dive to dive. Grapes are harvested from August to early October (aka "crush season") and the area is crawling with tourists. The best time to go is the first two weeks of November, when the grapes have settled and the fake winos go back to drinking corner store bottles. There are many ways to get to wine country, the easiest (but not the cheapest) of which is to book a tour that leaves from SF. Many different tours

are available and most will pick you up from where you're staying or arrange a meeting location for the group. You can also take a ferry to Vallejo (from Pier 41 or the Ferry Building) and book your trip from there. Put on your grown-up pants and prepare to hop around wineries, learn some grape history, and get tipsy on the good stuff.

SAUSALITO/MARIN

Sausalito and Marin Counties are just across the Golden Gate Bridge, but seem worlds away. These are communities that have fought against condo development and gentrification and won. Sausalito is known for its houseboat (rather, "floating home") community and you can take a walking tour around the colorful boat homes. Sausalito is also home base for Heath Ceramics, an artisan tableware company. You can walk into the factory after 11 a.m. on weekends for a tour. Marin is known for small bakeries, crafty

food, mom-and-pop diners, old-school shops, quaint cafés, the impeccable collection of redwoods found in Muir Woods, and the time the Grateful Dead spent living here from 1975 to 1995. Both towns may have an isolationist mentality, but that's what's kept them unique.

BIG SUR

Big Sur is a spectacular clash of mountains and sea along the California coastline. You'll want to rent a car for this one for the full effect and drive straight down the 101 Highway for about three hours. Once there, you'll be hit in the face with green rolling hills, coastal redwood trees, waterfalls that spill into the ocean, and the kind of roads you see in car commercials (which are actually taped here). You can reserve a campsite at Pfeiffer Big Sur State Park for $35, then nature-hike until your lungs explode from ODing on fresh air.

BURNING MAN

In 1986, two dudes expressed their freedom to burn shit down by erecting a giant wooden man and setting him aflame on Baker Beach in the Presidio. This annual tradition grew in size, and in 1996 the police deemed it a fire hazard and forced the fest elsewhere. Burning Man went from the beach to Black Rock (Nevada), a vast, dried-out lakebed surrounded by nothing but sand for miles. Referred to as "the Playa," the location, push for creative expression, and lack of authority or regulation led to an explosion of fest-goers (aka burners). The new incarnation of the festival is a week-long event (beginning the last Monday of August), and one for which artists, dancers, musicians, and hallucinogen-lovers prepare for all year. It's an experience you have to have once, and San Francisco hooks you up with all the tools. Every thrift shop will have the glittery booty shorts and requisite

desert goggles, and hitching a ride is as easy as asking around. Tickets are $380 and released in limited quantities, and you can apply for a low-income 50 percent discount. This is serious party business.

OTP Tip: If you return to SF from the Playa with some serious burner jet lag, Decompression is a rave that goes down in SOMA to help ease your post–Burning Man blues.

YOSEMITE NATIONAL PARK

A protected piece of American wilderness, Yosemite is known for its huge waterfalls, ancient sequoia trees, and heart-stopping views. For an introduction to the beauty, drive in through the Wawona Tunnel, which opens up into a picturesque view of cliffs, trees, and mountains that seem to go on forever. You can spend the day hiking its many trails, camping, feeding ducks, and exploring the trunks of some of the oldest trees in the country. The entrance fee is $20 for cars and $10 on foot (free on select dates; check Nps.gov) and is good for a seven-day pass to the park.

LAKE TAHOE

A three-hour drive from the city, Lake Tahoe is an excellent snowboarding destination. The Heavenly Resort is open starting November 21 and goes until the last day of the season. It has amazing trails for all skill levels, and if you wipe out, the powder is soft enough to keep your coccyx intact. One-day passes are a reasonable $99 and you can save on lodging by staying in a dorm at Hostel Tahoe for $30 a night. When you're done playing in the snow, hop over to nearby Reno, Nevada, for some debaucherous gambling in the grimier, de-glitzed version of Vegas.

AUTHOR BIOS

ANNA STAROSTINETSKAYA

Anna is the editor-in-chief of *Off Track Planet* and has been happily in charge of content production from day one. Born in the former USSR, Anna has a passion for travel that began early in life when her family left the Union, first stopping in Austria and Italy, before settling in Los Angeles in 1990. After a long stint in LA, Anna moved to Brooklyn in 2009 and cofounded Off Track Planet. She spent six winters pulling icicles from her hair until moving to San Francisco in 2015.

FREDDIE PIKOVSKY

Freddie is the CEO of Off Track Planet and has his hands in every aspect of the company. After backpacking through Europe in 2008, he moved to a hostel in Brooklyn, where he started Off Track Planet. Freddie is responsible for the creative direction of this guide book. He recently completed a road trip across the U.S. on a vintage motorcycle and will be backpacking around the world in 2015. Freddie would like to specially thank Anna Homsey for her unconditional support throughout this crazy journey.

ACKNOWLEDGMENTS

We'd like to thank everyone who made this guide possible. Thank you for opening your doors and letting us crash on your couches, and for giving us interesting suggestions and taking the time to discuss local politics. Thank you to the cafés that didn't evict us from our temporary coffices and the proprietor of HRD for giving us extra kiwi salad dressing, just so we could try it. Thanks to the people who kept up with our bar hopping in the name of maximizing coverage, and the MUNI bus drivers who helped us navigate around this city's web of wheels. To all the people we met on this exploratory journey through San Francisco, thank you for showing us the corners, crevices, and quirks that make your city so awesomely bizarre.

A special thank-you to photographers Ian Lundie, Greg Crespo, Kevin Block Photography, and "Kennejima."

PHOTO CREDITS

p. 5: Kevin Edwards; pp. 6, 19 (bottom), 94: John, aka Star5112; p. 8: Alice Brown Chittenden; p. 9 (Jedediah Smith): unknown friend of Smith; p. 9 (James Marshall): public domain; p. 9 (earthquake): U.S. National Archives; p. 10 (Al Capone): Federal Bureau of Prisons; p. 10 (Golden Gate Bridge): Mr. Euler; p. 10 (Jack Kerouac): Tom Palumbo; p. 11 (Summer of Love): Ian Parkes; p. 11 (Apple): Rama & Musée Bolo; p. 11 (Google): Shawn Collins; pp. 13 (left), 23 (bottom right), 25 (top right), 26, 37 (right), 39, 40, 53, 54 (bottom), 55, 56, 57 (left), 58 (bottom right), 64, 77, 78 (top and center), 81 (right), 83 (right), 88, 89 (center & bottom), 90, 93 (right), 95, 96, 97, 101 (left), 102 (bottom photos), 103, 107, 110, 111, 114 (middle), 125 (left), 126 (bottom), 127 (left), 130, 132, 137 (left), 147, 149 (bottom), 157 (bottom), 163 (right), 165 (bottom), 172, 174, 199 (top right & bottom right), 200 (left), 202, 203 (top & middle), 204 (left), 205 (left), 206, 214, 216, 217, 223 (top right), 224, 225 (bottom), 226: Freddie Pikovsky; p. 14: Mobilus In Mobili; pp. 15 (naked bikers), 213 (top): Eric Molina; pp. 15 (bike store), 113 (left): Dustin Jensen; p. 15 (stairs): Lorena Flores; p. 16: Helder Ribeiro; pp. 18, 21, 171 (left): Scott Richard; p. 19 (top): Anthony Quintano; p. 23 (top two images), 51 (left), 58 (left-side images), 145 (left), 155 (bottom), 156, 182 (left, middle top, & bottom): Kevin Block Photography; p. 23 (bottom loft): Jennifer Woodard Maderazo; pp. 25 (left), 104 (left), 209 (left); Evan Blaser; pp. 25 (bottom right), 27, 31, 32, 33, 35, 37 (left), 38, 40 (left), 41, 47, 68, 69, 100 (right), 101 (right), 104 (right), 112, 117, 153: Greg Crospo; p. 29: Britt Selvitelle; p. 30: Jen blu_pineappl3; pp. 34, 43, 164 (left), 166 (bottom), 225 (top): Rick and Richard Audet; pp. 42 (top), 98, 128 (top): Charles Haynes; p. 42 (bottom): AgentAkit; pp. 44, 45, 46, 93 (left), 107 (bottom), 114 (bottom), 171 (right), 178 (right), 179, 182 (top & middle bottom), 228: Ian Lundie; pp. 49, 207 (top): Scott Richard, aka torbakhopper; p. 51 (right): Phil Whitehouse; p. 52 (left): alcuin lai, p. 52 (right): Atlaslin; p. 54 (top): Daigo Tanaka; p. 57 (right): David Silry, p. 59: Nick Fullerton; p. 61 (left): Wonderlane; p. 61 (right): Jérôme Decq; pp. 62, 63, 175 (right), 178 (left), 191 (right), 215 (top): Cory Stevens; p. 65: PunkToad; p. 67 (top): Kevin McCarthy; p. 67 (bottom): Gordon Wrigley; p. 70: Angelo DeSantis; p. 71: Scott Schiller; p. 73: Zooy Kroll; pp. 13 (right), 74, 83 (left), 126 (top), 136, 160, 162, 163 (left), 165 (top), 200 (right), 215 (bottom): kennejimar; p. 75 (top): Duncan Hull; p. 75 (bottom): Christopher Bowns; pp. 76, 124: Arnold Gatilao; pp. 78 (bottom), 148 (bottom): Sonny Abesamis; p. 79 (top): Jun Seita; p. 79 (bottom), 116 (left), Ann Larie Valentino; p 81 (left): Tony Webster; p. 82 (left): jencu; p. 82 (right): Pacific P; p. 84: Rick Audet; p. 85 (top): Maria Ly; p. 85 (bottom): Becky Snyder; pp. 86 (top), 140, 177 (top): David McSpadden; pp. 86 (bottom), 87, 129 (right): Kārlis Dambrāns; p. 89 (top): Don DeBold; pp. 91, 115 (top), 137 (right): Christopher Michel; p. 99: Hillary Hartley; pp. 100 (left), 116 (right): Gaelen; p. 102 (top): Incase; p. 105: Jules Morgan; p. 106: Chuck Heston; p. 108: 7oxcleb; pp. 109 (left), 219 (top & middle): Davity Dave; p. 109 (right): Nicholas Boos; p. 113 (right): Barb Howe; pp. 114 (top), 184 (right): Orin Zebest; p. 115 (bottom): Todd Anderson; p. 118: Michela/UTW/Mik; p. 119 (left): Daniel 7emans; p 119 (right): Dolores Park Works; pp. 120, 150 (top): Charles Nadeau; p. 123 (left): Nan Palmero; p. 123 (right): Glen Scarborough; p. 125 (right), markheybo; pp. 127 (right), 139: T.Tseng; pp. 128 (middle & bottom), 193 (top): stu_spivack; pp. 66, 129 (left): Marcin Wichary; p. 131 (left): Michael Albov; pp. 131 (right), 229 (right): Tom Hilton; pp. 133, 232 (bottom): Jennifer Morrow; p. 135 (left): BluePics; p. 135 (right): Chris Hunkeler; p. 138 (left): Chris Martin, p. 138 (right): Jay Cross; pp. 48, 141, 142 (right), 231 (bottom): Matt Baume; p. 142 (left): Krista, aka goodieshrst; p. 143: Mary aka swimfinfan; p. 145 (right): Bob Hall; pp. 146, 149 (top), 169: Alejandro De La Cruz; p. 148: (top): Rachel Hathaway; p. 148 (middle): DJHeini, p. 149 (middle): mizlit; pp. 150, 204 (top right): sekimura; p. 204 (bottom right): Ludovic Bertron; p. 205 (right): torroid; p. 207 (bottom): Cliffords Photography; p. 208: Pierre Phaneuf; p. 209 (right): Aaron Muszalski; p. 211 (left): James Cohen; p. 211 (top right): Sharon Mollerus; p. 211 (bottom right): The Wandering Angel; p. 212: Fifty/Fifty; p. 213 (bottom): Danielle Scott; p. 219 (bottom): Kevin Krejci; p. 220 (right): Dave Fayram; p. 220 (left): Franco Folini; p. 221 (top): Michael Fraley; p. 223 (left): Laura Brunow Miner; p. 223 (bottom right): Joe Mabel; p. 227: Christina Xu; p. 229 (left): Oskari Kettunen; p. 230: Alex Torrenegra; p. 231: Matthias Klappenbach; p. 232 (top): Brandon "BPPrice"; p. 233: David Sanabria